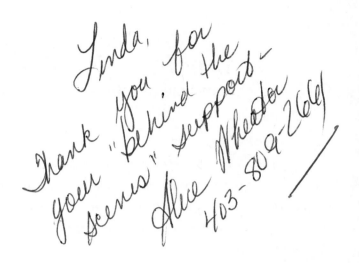
Linda,
Thank you for
your "behind the
scenes" support –
Alice Wheeler
403-809-2669

Imperfect
Forgiveness

"Through reading *Imperfect Forgiveness; the Miracle of Releasing Hurt Bit by Bit!* I have come to realize that forgiveness is an ongoing process that calms my way and lightens my load. If you own this book you will refer to it many times throughout your lifetime."

—**Gary McKelvie,** Senior Account Manager, Commercial Real Estate

"Alice provides practical steps that help people gain inner peace. The more we have of inner peace the higher our vibration. Consequently, the more of the good things we will attract into our life. I appreciate her straight forward style and the sincere heart behind it..."

—**Jannette Anderson,** President,
Chief Marketing Strategist, Positive Results

"I really enjoyed your concept of learning to find compassion for the person who has wronged us as a step towards forgiveness. I think that if we all were humble enough to realize that we are not perfect and need others to forgive us that perhaps we could then realize the importance of forgiving others. If we can't forgive, how can we expect to be forgiven?"

—**Janice M. Elmquist,** Lawyer, Calgary, Alberta

"Too often people let betrayal and its consequential hurt, anger and resentment eat away at them. Wheaton offers a sound process to give relief. Forgivers live with freedom and peace. I will be recommending this book to my clients and those lost in blame."

—**Patricia Morgan,** Counselor, Speaker and author of the bestseller,
Love Her as She Is: Lessons From A Daughter Stolen By Addictions

"Alice has offered a workable and real process for forgiving others. Following her process allows us to be who we are inside and to make the world a happier place."

—**Rosemary Walter,** Mosaic Marketing Management, Inc.,
Arlington Heights, Illinois

Imperfect
Forgiveness

The miracle of releasing hurt bit by bit

Alice Wheaton

NEW YORK

Imperfect Forgiveness
The miracle of releasing hurt bit by bit

Disclaimer: The Publisher and the Author make no representations or warranties with respect to the accuracy or completeness of the contents of this work and specifically disclaim all warranties, including without limitation warranties of fitness for a particular purpose. No warranty may be created or extended by sales or promotional materials. The advice and strategies contained herein may not be suitable for every situation. This work is sold with the understanding that the Publisher is not engaged in rendering legal, accounting, or other professional services. If professional assistance is required, the services of a competent professional person should be sought. Neither the Publisher nor the Author shall be liable for damages arising herefrom. The fact that an organization or website is referred to in this work as a citation and/or a potential source of further information does not mean that the Author or the Publisher endorses the information the organization or website may provide or recommendations it may make. Further, readers should be aware that internet websites listed in this work may have changed or disappeared between when this work was written and when it is read.

ISBN 978-1-60037-778-5 paperback
ISBN 978-1-61448-293-2 eBook
Library of Congress Control Number: 2010925910

Morgan James Publishing
The Entrepreneurial Publisher
5 Penn Plaza, 23rd Floor,
New York City, New York 10001
(212) 655-5470 office • (516) 908-4496 fax
www.MorganJamesPublishing.com

Cover Design by:
Chris Treccani
www.3dogdesign.net

Interior Design by:
Bonnie Bushman
bonnie@caboodlegraphics.com

In an effort to support local communities, raise awareness and funds, Morgan James Publishing donates a percentage of all book sales for the life of each book to Habitat for Humanity Peninsula and Greater Williamsburg.

Get involved today, visit
www.MorganJamesBuilds.com.

DEDICATION

To all my family, I dedicate this book and extend an offer of gratitude for their input into my life. My mother, Jane Wheaton, placed an emphasis on my education and learning which I will carry with me always. She was a fierce protector for which I am very grateful – God help anyone who came between her and her children! Newton Wheaton, my beloved father, provided comfort, and encouragement in our weekly conversations. He was the most forgiving and accepting person I knew. His joy and abundant spirit showed on his face and in his actions towards his family and his community. He modeled unconditional love, acceptance, forgiveness, and unbridled trust in the universe. My brother, Earl Wheaton, taught me how speak up for myself and be more assertive than I was inclined at the time. My brother, Lloyd Wheaton, was my childhood hero. He taught me to swim, to skate, and to fish! I still recall coming home from fishing *at the steady* with my bamboo fishing pole and my precious catch of trout. Moreover, he was part of the inspiration for me to write this book.

CONTENTS

FOREWORD

by Kim Phuc
(*The Girl in the Vietnam War Picture*)

Congratulations Alice, on writing an inspiring book about a fundamental issue in the world. Peace and forgiveness are two elements that are often overlooked when measuring success and progress. Peace and forgiveness are the cornerstones of peace of mind. In order to have peace of mind, one must sincerely offer and accept the kind of authentic forgiveness that supersedes understanding. The precepts outlined in your book clearly detail how individuals can work towards attaining peace of mind.

I rely on the strength given to me through Jesus Christ to forgive and subsequently love my enemies, just as the Lord has forgiven and loves me. I believe that the peace of mind I live with is a result of God changing my heart.

Kim making a presentation to a conference in Luxembourg, September 19-21, 2003, on the International Day of Peace.

I applaud you for writing this book. Forgiveness and peace are highly sought after commodities. The world will be much better off when all of us have all read your book and sincerely seek to offer and accept authentic forgiveness that supersedes understanding.

—**Kim Phuc,** Founder,
The Kim Foundation International

ACKNOWLEDGEMENTS

Several angels helped with both the editing and the organization of this book. The first person I would like to thank is Peggy Wall. Not only did Peggy read, re-read, and provide feedback on the first draft of the book, but she also co-opted a member of her book club to do so as well. She offered further encouragement by insisting on being the first person to purchase the book. I would like to thank Susan Lorimer for her gracious willingness to read and review a book for someone she had never met. This still amazes me. Cindy LaValley went from being a participant in a workshop I was leading to an editing angel.

I want to thank Liz Corbier who provides professional services with her Office and Home Maintenance company and has become a great friend as well. Celeste Peters is an editor extraordinaire and I feel deep gratitude for her help. Her insight into the human condition, combined with her knowledge of what contributes to great writing, was a powerful combination.

Lori King, Elaine Evans, Tracy Sherba, Jannette Anderson, and Lavana Fitzgerald are also long-term friends and I appreciate our history!

I wish to acknowledge my son, Lloyd Worth, for his wit and excellent style of mirroring back to me the work that I do. He is the air that I breathe and my heart is more open because of him.

My son Lloyd Worth is the light of my life and his support in getting this work into the world via Multi Media gives me hope, energy, and renewed inspiration. His intelligence and keen interest on current affairs and politics keeps me engaged in conversation with the worldview from a 20+ year old perspective!

Many years ago, when I was a very young and naïve woman, I met, loved, and married Andy Sherwood. Even though we went our separate ways, I continued to recall and recite his wit and wisdom. Twenty-eight years later, due to a series of coincidences, we reconnected, developed a strong friendship, and are living examples of the power of *Imperfect Forgiveness*. Andy, I am grateful for your unfailing support in the work that I do.

The final angel was Darlene Hull, social media expert extraordinaire, who read the manuscript with three highlighters to identify three different key points. Orange was for changes, blue for blog topics, and green for Twitter statements. Knowing about Social Media is not my expertise but having a friend and expert make it easier for me is out of this world…truly angelic. Thank you Darlene!

THE KIM FOUNDATION

The concept of the Kim Foundation was inspired by Kim Phuc, an innocent victim of the Vietnam War at the age of nine. On June 8, 1972, Kim's village of Trang Bang came under attack by South Vietnamese planes, which mistakenly dropped napalm on a Buddhist pagoda in an area the North Vietnamese were infiltrating. While running for safety with other children, Kim was severely burned by the napalm.

The Kim Foundation's mission is to help heal the wounds suffered by innocent children, and to restore hope and happiness to their lives by providing much needed medical and psychological assistance.

For information contact:
The Kim Phuc Foundation
P.O. Box 31025, 475 Westney Road North
Ajax, Ontario, CANADA L1T 3V2
www.kimfoundation.com

INTRODUCTION

*W*HEN ANGER AND RESENTMENT EAT
AWAY AT YOU, HOW CAN THERE BE ROOM TO
EXPERIENCE JOY?

Moving Out of Fear

There are simple strategies to help you move away from hurt and move towards peace of mind, and the purpose of this book is to present them to you. After all, what good is wealth if resentment slowly eats us alive, resulting in both physical and emotional debilitating illnesses? Even if our illnesses and emotional issues are not life threatening, they can be life limiting. What good is power if we do not have power over our own perceptions and reactions to life?

We will have a constant ache and hunger in our hearts if we are unable to freely give and receive love. We cannot change the past but we can claim the future we desire by using the hunger in our hearts, the power of our minds, and the strength of our mental and emotional beings to propel us forward. Change, even a good change that takes us from feelings of fear, doubt, and insecurity to feelings of light, love, and peace, can be difficult to master. The human condition appears to desire holding on to the comfort zone despite strong desires to achieve something more.

There are secrets, steps, and strategies for working with this information. In many cases, you do not have to do anything except change your mind to be free from emotional pain. This book will not burden your life by expecting you to take time out of your busy schedule. Just reading the book may be enough to make all of the difference.

The ideas discussed in this book have a high degree of emotional content, and yet it is set up in a prescriptive format – four steps for one problem and three steps to handle another, and so on. Emotional issues can be improved if they are dealt with rationally. That is not to say the rational systems will remove all of the pain, anger, and resentment of the past; however, the right system can reduce the negative impact these feelings have on your life now and in the future. These emotionally charged issues provide a rationale and a system for resolution. By reading this book, you will have a strong start on learning how to practice the four kinds of forgiveness:

1. Forgive a perpetrator and repair broken trust
2. Forgive yourself
3. Ask for forgiveness from others whom you have hurt
4. Ask God or your Higher Power for forgiveness/help
   with forgiving

Peace in the world will come about much faster when we have the capacity to go internal, to the place of discord, and shift those painful thoughts and feelings ever so slightly. It is not as if we have to change one hundred and eighty degrees overnight. Real and lasting changes occur over time, somewhat like a ratchet wrench that tightens a fraction with each twist.

Developing New Skills

In learning the four types of forgiveness, you will be introduced to new ways of thinking which will require a completely new skill set. The following are the top ten new skills you will learn as part of this process:

- Move from Judgment (limited) to Discernment (expansive).
- Develop compassion and know what it is, and is not.
- Completely understand and eliminate defensive behavior.
- Practice the four types of forgiveness.
- Recover from fear of confrontation.
- Tell almost anyone almost anything.
- Release the hurt and discover the lesson.
- Develop one hundred percent trustworthiness.
- Move from victim to victory.
- Develop a courteous heart where happiness is a constant companion.

For instance, I have deliberately presented the book in a prescriptive format because I have spent so much of my life searching for answers. Like you, I needed answers because my relationships were not as smooth as I believed they deserved to be. When there were relationship disappointments, either personal or professional, my peace of mind was compromised and I felt unhappy. I spent too much time confused by my own big reactions, and the reactions of others, to seemingly small events. I noticed that most of my issues were because of a missed communication;

either communication did not occur at all or it occurred in a non-supportive manner.

Then I began to put into place formulas, steps, or as I call them, prescriptions for personal communication. These prescriptions have helped me to find my answers.

Finding answers to many of life's questions:

- How can I tell the truth of an issue to someone I care about, in a way that will not hurt them and yet be fair and respectful to myself?
- How can I tell my truth to someone I fear and still be safe?
- How can I ask for what I want with equanimity and grace?
- How can I make a mistake, make amends for that, and still be liked and respected?
- What is the opposite of being a victim?
- Why are the feelings of fear, doubt, and insecurity ever-present?
- How can I overcome the fear of confrontation?
- How can I not respond to attack with attack?
- How can I create healthy boundaries?
- Why do I sometimes trust the untrustworthy?
- Why must I forgive?
- How can I forgive and move on? What steps must I take?
- What separates winners from whiners?
- How can I be sure I am spiritual enough?
- How can I be someone that inspires respect and admiration in others?
- How can I be sure to reach my potential?
- How can I tap into the good graces of others?
- What options exist for me if I feel threatened? Do I have to respond with fight or flight?

- Is there a better way to go through life?

For instance, the simple step of asking for permission to share something with another made all of the difference! It ensured that they were willing to be attentive to my question and consider my request. I learned that saying, "Let me ask you a question," softens an otherwise difficult question. It created receptivity and the person with whom I was speaking actually waited, became silent, and created a space and gave attention to the forthcoming question.

A similar reaction, receptivity, occurred when I began to give people a choice by saying a version of, "What I would like to do, if it's alright with you ..." Preparing my exchanges in this manner made my life easier. I no longer had to posture or jockey for position. Life began to work out in the process of life itself.

I have had prolonged periods of peace of mind and I wanted to let others, who may be similarly confused by the above questions, to have the same experience of life as supportive and rewarding as I have come to have. Therefore, I wrote this book.

I hope you can identify with at least one of the prescriptions herein. If not, please forgive me and know that if not now, then maybe sometime in the future you may find yourself in a delicate position, in need of an answer. This can become your reference book!

Your opinion matters to me. I am very interested in hearing from my readers, whatever your opinion. Feel free to communicate with me by emailing me at alice@alicewheaton.com.

Chapter 1

FORGIVENESS AND PEACE OF MIND

*O*UR PEACE OF MIND IS MORE PRECIOUS THAN WEALTH AND POWER. NONE OF THE MONEY IN THE WORLD CAN BUY PEACE OF MIND AND WITHOUT IT OUR EMOTIONAL AND PHYSICAL HEALTH SUFFERS.

The journey to inner peace

Forgiveness is a hot topic today. This may be because we are searching for peace in the chaos and unhappiness that hangs over society. Forgiveness, as defined by *Webster's New International Dictionary*, is to cease to feel resentment against another on account of a wrong committed. It makes sense then that the opposite of forgiveness is resentment. The dictionary's definition of resentment is "anger and ill will in view of real or fancied wrong". Those real or perceived wrongs may have occurred years ago and the perpetrator might not even recall the event, yet we carry all that anger, resentment and blame for years. Any healer, either mystical or medical, will alert clients to the dangers and rampant damage caused by these feelings.

Imagine a garden watering can sitting for a few days with just a teaspoon of battery acid added to the water inside. That watering can will degrade and irreparable damage occurs. Holding resentment, blame, and anger, wreaks similar havoc on the core of our being.

It is easier to be right than to be happy. When we hold resentment towards another, we justify and defend our position, maintain our rightness, and carve a niche of superiority for ourselves. This position of needing to be right circumvents happiness and holds us in a cradle of false-superiority. We take comfort in this feeling of being superior to friends, family, co-workers, neighbors, etc. The self-righteousness that we nurture when we hold ourselves in a superior position to others is the constant companion of resentment. This deadly combination of self-righteousness and resentment is a fortress keeping love, passion, and the juiciness of life at a distance.

This fortress prevents our hearts from receiving and sharing a wide, varied, and full expression of the offerings life has to offer. It is as if we have guards positioned around our hearts, standing at attention and demanding that there be *nothing in; nothing out.* Sadly, because our hearts and minds have held resentment and anger for a prolonged time, this defended and limited state feels normal.

The anger I am talking about is not a quick burst of emotion but the deep abiding anger that usually accompanies a thirst for revenge. It lays a figurative yoke of blame and shame around the neck of the perpetrator. This deep-seated anger isolates.

What does it take to move from feeling resentment toward someone to forgiving that person? The solution is easier than you might think. Although the timing may differ for everyone, the process is similar.

Aside from feeling peace of mind, there are other benefits to releasing resentment. As an example, let us view our heart as a container that has the capacity to hold ten gallons of emotion. When resentment, anger, and fear occupy eight gallons, there is only room for two gallons of love. A diminished life is the result of a heart compromised by hanging onto fears, hurts, and resentments. You cannot fill a ten-gallon bucket with gold and diamonds when it is already filled with sand and rocks!

More than ever before, people are becoming dissatisfied with working for corporations. Instead, they want to fulfill their spiritual mission on earth, find their life purpose. It is difficult to imagine how awareness of one's life mission and the love and care from others, can be claimed by a heart filled with the grittiness of resentment. This is sad, but true. The extent that you harbor resentment in your heart and mind is the extent to which you are keeping love, peace, generosity, and joy, at bay.

For those who practice an attitude of forgiveness, life's greatness shows up in the process of life itself. This does not mean that we tolerate the intolerable and accept the unacceptable without life-preserving boundaries. It means that we have a forgiving heart and that we filter our reactions to life, and the people in our life, through that process.

At this point, you may want to reflect on your life and your attitudes, and wonder if there is room in your heart to forgive the indignities of the past and receive more of everything that life wants to deliver to you, now and in the future. Harboring the last vestiges of resentment may be the stone blocking your door to health, happiness, prosperity, and love.

There are four types of forgiveness that most people will need to seek in this lifetime:

1. Seeking God's forgiveness
2. Forgiving others
3. Forgiving yourself
4. Seeking the forgiveness of others

The first is God's (or your version of a Higher Power's) forgiveness. The second is the forgiveness of others for their real or imagined infractions towards us. Third, we need to seek the forgiveness of ourselves for our own imperfect path towards our destiny. The fourth, and most difficult bridge of forgiveness to cross, is helping others to forgive us of our transgressions towards them. This is a very difficult stage because it requires us to feel vulnerable. You can complete the first three processes of forgiveness in private. Rejection, and the resultant uncomfortable feelings, is a very real possibility when we "go public" and seek others' forgiveness. Asking for forgiveness is important to releasing the past – it helps us come full circle. In the process, the burden of shame and guilt lifts and self-esteem and confidence are restored again.

We hear about the Power of Forgiveness but we do not hear *how* to forgive, except to pray for them. This is a powerful position to take but problems still arise. We may not be prayerfully inclined and the resentments linger. The potential sounds promising but you may be someone who is desperate for relief now. The processes in this book will give you that immediate relief.

Hand in hand, with forgiveness is the importance of forgetting the anger and hurts from the distant or recent past. Forgetting is vital because to remember the past is to re-injure one's self and to be stuck there. Without forgetting, there is no peace of mind. Without peace of mind, there is bondage to others. This bondage is to be in *victim* mode, to have both one's peace of mind and present life affected by others. Life is too short and the consequences too harsh not to move on. "That was then and this is now," can become one of the phrases we use to jolt ourselves out of the past. Ruminating about those unhappy days keeps resentment and hurt activated. Anyone in the grip of resentment suffers emotional, physical, and spiritual isolation. That is a high price to pay for holding onto painful memories and inner rage.

The idea is to live with peace of mind, to go through life without defenses or pretenses. This guarantees that we stay open to all the opportunities life has to offer. If your heart and mind have an emotional capacity of ten gallons, fill the entire capacity with peace and possibilities rather than with resentment and rage.

Some people have been outraged when I suggest that they forgive a person for a wrong. Sometimes the reaction is disbelief. Their comments include, "No, he/she does not deserve forgiveness!" One person was so enraged with me during a workshop based on this book, that she stormed out of the room and her last words before she slammed the door were, "Some things and some people are unforgivable!"

This comment led to a hearty debate. There were conflicting opinions and attitudes but as we worked through the dynamics this declaration had created, the consensus was: *yes, everything can be forgiven, but not everything can be condoned or forgotten.*

That is a common mistake – to think that to forgive the unthinkable is to condone the unthinkable. Nothing could be further from the truth. We must forgive because there is no other way to feel the deep peace that comes from the strength of our core. If we cannot rebuild our core, we are destined to feel discord in all areas of our life. Moreover, how can we possibly influence world peace if there is no peace inside each of us?

Forgiveness is the answer to inner peace and world peace. Saying, "I will only forgive persons A, B, and C but resent, judge and blame persons D, E, and F," is not a winning formula. We must be willing to have at least one percent forgiveness for every person or circumstance that stimulates fear, anger, and resentment. When you take this stand, you will take life on life's terms instead of trying to control the people, events, and circumstances over which you have no control.

One percent seems like a small shift and it is, but let me assure you again, you and therefore by association your world, will experience the quantum positive results experienced by your peace of mind.

CHAPTER II

REASONS NOT TO FORGIVE

CONSTANTLY RUMINATING ABOUT THE PERSON WHO HURT US MEANS WE ARE OBSESSED AND POSSESSED. LIFE TAKES ON A GRAYISH BROWN HUE, RATHER THAN THE BRILLIANCE OF A RAINBOW.

The Power of Forgiveness

The tendency for negative thinking, criticism of others, and a fatalistic, catastrophic mindset about the future, is the dark side. Without forgiveness, we are destined to live and die in the outfields of life. To the extent that we forgive is the extent to which we are liberated from the dungeon in our mind. Coming to the point of forgiveness is easier if we are willing to take a leap of faith. *Blind faith* is when we believe we already have the power to change, and we begin to modify behaviors and attitudes even though we have no evidence. Blind faith has its seed in hope. Hope, like fear, is always about the future. Without hope, all is lost. However, hope alone gets us nowhere. To bring out the best in ourselves, and to bring out the best in others, we need to combine hope with action.

The power of forgiveness is unsurpassed. When we act as if we have the power to forgive, confidence develops and we experience forgiveness moments, one after another. A person who forgives and accepts others eventually learns to forgive and accept his or her own self. It is important to see everyone, including ourselves, as works in progress.

I cannot know me unless I look into your eyes and see me there. Knowing and accepting you as separate and distinct, yet part of the imperfect unity of humanity, means I can observe your behavior without removing myself from you. This is my understanding of the term *loving detachment*. It means I can stand back and observe *what is so* in a lovingly detached manner, rather than becoming hooked by any little drama you create. I can ask myself, "What is the problem/drama? Whose problem or drama is it? How does it serve me to become part of this drama?"

Hurt People Hurt People

We generally recognize that forgiveness is necessary for us to move forward. Authors and television hosts regularly discuss the value of forgiveness and this kind of dialogue has tremendous merit. However, they rarely teach a concrete, systematic approach to making amends when we make a mistake. Nor is there a process that allows us to forgive others who offend us. We are told to forgive and to be responsible for healing the relationship, but doing so is usually a long and arduous path. One reason for that difficulty, I believe, is our society extols the virtue of forgiving but does not provide a process to follow. We are repeatedly encouraged to forgive and to turn the other cheek, but that is easier said than done, especially when our emotions and vulnerabilities cause us to feel so raw.

Another message I would like every reader to understand is: As sure as others have injured us, we have injured others and are, ourselves, in need of forgiveness. In addition, many people say and do things to themselves that they would never allow a stranger to say and do to them. Because we have been abusive toward ourselves, we must put ourselves at or very near the top of our amends list. We must learn to forgive ourselves.

When things are going well, do you ever do something to sabotage all the good coming your way? Could it be that sabotaging your own best efforts is a direct result of bringing your inner frustrations to the surface? Could it be your higher self, telling you that you must take care of your inner landscape before you map out your full potential and reap the outward benefits?

If there is joy in your heart, it will surely show on your face. However, that joy remains hidden if it is layered over with the many faces of fear. Sadly, without releasing your resentment and anger, you may never experience your own joy and abundant spirit, or be able to share it with others. Forgiveness favors the face! A spirited self has abundant energy, creativity, and personality. Resentment is such a waste of a good spirit.

No doubt, people have hurt us. Sometimes we are victimized through no fault of our own by someone we perceive to be mean, angry, or violent. Why would we categorize another person as such? Because when we resent another person we evaluate his or her character in comparison to our own, and we always find the other person wanting. This process cannot occur without us feeling superior. We believe we would never do, say, or act like the person upon whom we sit in judgment.

Gossiping is another way to position ourselves as superior. We judge and condemn others based on mere speculation and then engage in character assassination. Gossip is a form of cheap bonding where, for a brief moment, we feel close to another person at the expense of someone else.

Here is a news flash: The people for whom we have resentments may not know about our pain, and they might not even care if they knew their actions have been hurtful. They are blithely going about their business and having a better life, and just knowing that eats away at us, growing even more resentment. Our plaintive cry becomes, "How could such a mean person have such a great life while I continue to suffer?" Considering the unhappiness we feel when resentment, anger, and blame are in our hearts, why do we not forgive easily and quickly? There are several reasons, and though they are simple to identify, they are not easy to eliminate.

The two main benefits of resentment are too powerful for most people to relinquish. The first benefit of resentment is judgment and the second is self-righteousness. Judgment – perceiving the other person as wrong, mean, or bad – causes us to compare that person unfavorably to ourselves. "She stole that promotion by bad-mouthing me at work," we say to ourselves, and the unspoken part of that sentence is, "I would never do that to her."

The second benefit, self-righteousness, is the virulent mixture of anger, hurt, and blame, frothing and brewing inside us. This violent inner rage becomes our focus, and helps us feel superior.

Little does a resentful person know that those feelings are actually negative motivators – they form a false energy because this creates a vicious cycle... there is never an end to them. Even if it were possible to get even, what remains is more resentment and the cycle widens, catching everyone in its net of destruction. Forgiveness, it seems, requires that we abandon the anger that has been our main source of fuel.

Five Reasons People Use so as Not to Forgive

Despite all the positive side effects of forgiving, people feel justified in not forgiving. They do this for five main reasons.

Reason #1: Forgiving versus Condoning

Some people believe that to forgive is to condone. However, that is not the case at all. We can be outraged by the act, yet detached from the person who caused the wrong.

Reason #2: Feeling Powerless

Energy gained from prolonged anger can make us feel powerful. Releasing this anger can cause us to feel powerless.

Reason #3: Projecting Pain

Painful experiences can cause resentment, anger, and blame to thrive. Forgiveness may not seem like an option because feelings of loss, hurt, confusion, grief, and vulnerability – the results of forgiving – are more difficult to grasp and experience than feelings of anger and rage. This is because we project anger and rage outward onto the perpetrator, whereas hurt, loss, and grief, are felt deeply within.

Who among us has not projected pain onto others from time to time? That is normal. When it happens, we admit our wrongdoing, make amends, and move on. What is abnormal is to become mired in pain without the ability to resolve it, without choice. Sadly, to some, being mired in resentment seems less difficult than pushing their consciousness and spirit to a higher level where they can fully experience the hurt, grieve it, and move on with life. Grief is a natural response to loss of security, safety, or well being. Anger and resentment are easy substitutes for this grief that we are unable to resolve.

Reason #4: Bad Things Will Happen

Some people believe that if they are forgiving they will allow bad things to happen to them and their loved ones. Nothing could be further from the truth. Being full of grace and equanimity actually means having the power to create boundaries, and to intervene when someone is harming them or a person they care about. Being a forgiving person helps create strength of character.

Reason #5: Inability to See the Past

A yearning for the past to be how we would like it to be can result in an inability to see past events as they actually happened. This keeps resentment and anger fuelled. Our search continues for the person we would have become if the hurt had not happened. Resentful people are constantly searching to make sense of those hurts. This causes them to feel disenfranchised or small in some way. Their self-esteem becomes lodged in that moment from the past. However, that was then and this is now, and neither then nor now is forever.

To be stuck in the fantasy of trying to undo the past, trying somehow to right it with resentment and hatred, is like being a Knight of the Round Table chasing but never finding the Holy Grail. That magic cup, the being we would have been without the hurt, does not exist. A happy present (and an even happier future) is ours when we develop the ability to forgive, forget, and move on. Whatever feelings we harbor over a long period, feelings of resentment and anger, or feelings of love and compassion, begin to feel normal. If we are going to be stuck on autopilot with our feelings, they may as well be productive.

The Cost of not Forgiving

There are many reasons to move beyond the issues of the past. There are consequences to holding on to resentment and staying stuck. Begin now to believe it is possible to claim your birthright – happiness, joy, love, and prosperity. Take a moment to ponder each of the following points. See which ones apply to you.

Reasons to move beyond the past:

1. Are you hyper-vigilant? Do you become angry with others who offend you even slightly? (Example: A driver who does not change lanes the way you think it should be done.)

2. Are you hypercritical of yourself? The chances of being critical of others are higher if the answer to this question is yes.

3. Do you have conversations in your head with others who are not in the room? In those conversations, are you always right?

4. Are you unable to confront issues in a way that allows you to have a strong, loving relationship?

5. Do you ruminate on little infractions and allow the little things to escalate into big issues?

6. Is truce more important than truth? Are you a people pleaser?

7. Are you unable to create and maintain boundaries?

8. Do you have a tendency to practice *tyranny of the weak*? Are you so sensitive that your feelings are close to the surface? Have you trained those around you to say only what you want to hear to avoid making you upset, mad or defensive? Hearing only what you want to hear ensures that you are living an illusion instead of the truth of reality.

9. Are you a perfectionist, sabotaged by procrastination?

10. Are you unwilling to be in situations where making mistakes or failing is possible?

11. Are you hyper-confrontational (which, paradoxically, stems from fear of confrontation)? Do you practice *tyranny of the aggressive?* Often these people are egomaniacs with an inferiority complex.

12. Do you have a tendency to maintain physical isolation?

13. Does resentment show on your face where instead of having laugh lines, you have frown lines? (No amount of expensive face creams can erase the lines and wrinkles that accompany a resentful heart!)

14. Do you experience consistent emotional isolation? Who would want to commit to or stay committed to, a resentful person?

15. Are you spiritually isolated? Think how difficult it is to force water through a pipe filled with debris. Coming home to ourselves and being in the flow of our goodness is difficult when we harbor defensiveness, resentment, and anger.

If we have built up a way of thinking and a way of living over the years, it will be uncomfortable to begin the process of *changing our mind.* This is because we have a human tendency to defend our position, beliefs, and attitudes on life, even if they no longer serve us anymore. However, if it were easy, we would all achieve enlightenment!

Chapter III

PERCEPTION

*O*UR PERSONAL ASSUMPTIONS CAN COLOR
A SITUATION SO THAT WE ARE PERCEIVING
REALITY FROM THE LIMITATION OF OUR SINGLE
VIEWPOINT. WHO MUST BE WRONG FOR US TO
BE RIGHT?

Perception is not always reality

Ending a standoff caused by resentment and anger generally requires one member of a partnership to make the first move. That might mean swallowing a big dose of pride.

Steve, a friend and business associate, told me a story about how his firm grip on pride and resentment was shaken loose. First, he fell off his bicycle and broke a few ribs. Later, when his ribs had healed, he slipped off a sidewalk and severely broke his ankle. Restored to health, he received news that he had prostate cancer and required a radical prostatectomy. With six days to prepare for surgery, he asked himself some tough questions. Foremost among them was, "Okay universe, what am I not getting? What lesson am I missing?"

After beginning to suspect that the universe was trying to tell him something important, his thoughts focused on his long deceased parents, and his brother with whom he had not spoken in ten years. Steve decided to take the first step towards reconciliation. He spent hours with relatives going back to his parents' past, and discovered that his conclusions about their parenting infractions were based on the perceptions of an elementary school-aged boy.

At that young age his decisions were founded on faulty logic and reason, formed without full knowledge of the facts. He had misinformed himself, judged his parents, and treated them as if his impressions were the unwavering truth. He had made decisions based on perceived wrongdoings. Consequently, he spent much of his adult life numbed by the pain of anger and resentment. Eventually, Steve came to believe that those emotions sapped him of his physical health, spiritual elegance, and peace of mind. When he admitted this to himself, the relationship with his estranged brother began to heal.

Anger and resentment are emotional burdens that are too heavy for most people to bear. They rob us of our emotional, mental, and physical health, along with our creativity and power.

Differing perceptions can influence how we view real-life situations. The value of your observations largely depends on your ability to be aware of your own beliefs, assumptions, prejudices, expectations, and judgments. In standing back, try to recognize that you bring all these things with you to any situation. Then you might find you can more easily acknowledge that your own view of the situation is not accurate for anyone but yourself. Your perception of any situation is largely limited by your own interpretation, which is formed by your own beliefs, assumptions, prejudices, expectations, and judgments. Taking time to learn about another person's beliefs, assumptions, prejudices, expectations, and judgments will enable you to see the situation as they do and identify more closely with their reality. You may not agree with or like their reality, but you will be able to understand the world from their point of view.

Your Perception Is Influenced by Each of These Factors

Having expectations of others that cannot/will not be met is asking to be hurt first and then resentful later.

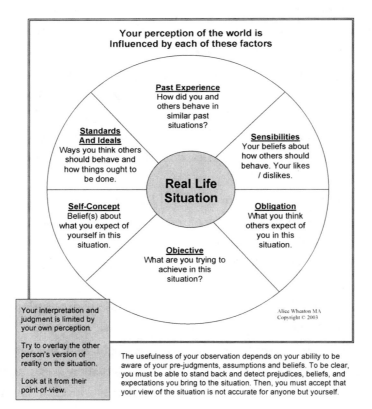

Your perception of the world is Influenced by each of these factors

Past Experience
How did you and others behave in similar past situations?

Standards And Ideals
Ways you think others should behave and how things ought to be done.

Sensibilities
Your beliefs about how others should behave. Your likes / dislikes.

Real Life Situation

Self-Concept
Belief(s) about what you expect of yourself in this situation.

Obligation
What you think others expect of you in this situation.

Objective
What are you trying to achieve in this situation?

Alice Wheaton M.A
Copyright © 2003

Your interpretation and judgment is limited by your own perception.

Try to overlay the other person's version of reality on the situation.

Look at it from their point-of-view.

The usefulness of your observation depends on your ability to be aware of your pre-judgments, assumptions and beliefs. To be clear, you must be able to stand back and detect prejudices, beliefs, and expectations you bring to the situation. Then, you must accept that your view of the situation is not accurate for anyone but yourself.

- Real-Life Situation
  What is it that you are experiencing right now? Are your expectations realistic or unrealistic? Do you feel at home in your body?
- Past Experience
  How have you and others behaved in similar situations in the past?
- Sensibilities
  How do you believe others should behave? Your likes/dislikes?
- Obligation
  What do you think others expect of you in this situation?
- Standards and Ideals
  Ways you think others should behave and how things ought to be done.
- Self-Concept
  Beliefs about what you expect of yourself in this situation.
- Objective
  What are you trying to achieve in this situation?

Someone who feels secure feels no need to project his or her anxieties onto others through criticism, irritability, or general intimidation.

The person on the receiving end of these forms of aggression, however, will frequently be intimidated, feel and act powerless. Essentially, these victims hand their power over to the aggressor, who is momentarily fortified and placated. The aggressor simply experiences cheap and transient self-esteem – cheap because it came at the expense of another's peace of mind, and transient because when self-esteem is stolen it cannot permanently be integrated into one's wholeness as a human being. Like an addict, a perpetrator must constantly have his or her supply. Soon the aggressor's desperate, craving search begins again and the cycle repeats itself, usually escalating until someone puts a stop to it.

You would think that the aggressor would feel deep remorse, not just transient remorse. Instead, the aggressor loses respect for the passive person and feels vindicated by the knowledge that the victim will allow this nasty behavior to continue. In turn, the victim often ups the ante, trying harder and harder to please the aggressor. Occasionally, but not in any predictable fashion, the victim will receive a small reward. It might be a brief acknowledgement or a coveted nod of approval. Since this positive reinforcement is usually non-specific, it causes the victim to renew efforts to please the aggressor. The victim's tolerance for criticism is beyond any semblance of normal expectation. It is as if the victim's agenda is to see how much abuse he or she can take before reaching the breaking point.

What power does a passive victim have? Plenty! Imagine the passive person kneeling with the dominant person's foot on his or her back. What happens if the passive person moves from the kneeling position? With the victim's back no longer available as a footrest, the aggressor will lose balance.

In most cases, however, the passive kneeling person is unaware of his or her power to shift the circumstances in one subtle move. The passive person maintains the power of martyrdom. The passive person projects the injustice of the situation by withdrawal and silence. The passive person may also be feeling a torrent of resentment and self-satisfaction caused by comparing the aggressor's mean behavior to his or her own sweetness, and then judging the aggressor to be wrong. In short, the victim gains cheap self-esteem because it comes from outside his or her core where someone else was the catalyst. Sourcing self-esteem from this way eventually creates a hungry heart and the feeling of having a hole in the soul.

Then, one day, one of them has an epiphany. A miracle occurs. One of them has an awakening and is able to see clearly the cyclical drama they have created. Someone moves. It may be the aggressive partner, no longer needing to acquire power by making the other person feel small. Alternatively, it may be the passive partner deciding not to kneel in supplication. Whatever the cause, benevolent power (as compared to caustic power) is given the opportunity to grow.

The path back to benevolent power will be rocky. The person who did not make the first move may feel abandoned, becoming angry at the partner who changed the rules of connection. Anger can be a source of self-protection but when left to simmer, it takes us hostage. Anger born out of resentment is one of the deadly sins because it leads to bitterness, cynicism, and constant complaints. It is important to discover if we are harboring any dark, abiding anger, and then find a way to get rid of it before it kills our souls.

Passivity is another one of the reactions to fear. Letting anger and resentment grow is a form of passivity. When we allow this passive response to remain, anger is strengthened.

When two people come together in forgiveness, there must also be a third. The third comes about through the transformation of both into a greater essence than either could be on their own. They are still persons A and B but they create an entirely new relationship, a third person if you will. Pause and ask yourself, "What am I willing to lose to maintain being right or righteous?"

When a wrong or injury occurs, emotions run high and our perceptions are negatively affected. If you have any negative, resentful feelings towards another person, take the time to discuss those feelings with the offender. Clean it up, and move on with the freedom to be what, or whom, you truly are – and truly are not.

Judgment versus Discernment is the Answer

The Chambers English Dictionary describes the word judgment as: *an opinion; pointing out or declaring what is just or law; passing sentence; comparing facts to determine the truth.* It describes the word discernment as: *the power or faculty of discriminating; thoroughly perceived; acuteness.*

To be in judgment is to view a person or situation as one-dimensional. It can be a positive or a negative judgment. *You are beautifully dressed,* is a judgment, a positive one. *You are a shabby dresser,* is also a judgment. In this book, however, when I refer to judgment I refer to the negative, limiting, one-dimensional thinking where an observer attaches a moral value to that which is being observed or perceived.

Discernment, on the other hand, looks at what is so without attaching a moral decision on the part of the observer. The astute, discerning observer is aware that his or her own perceptions play a big role in deciding the truth of any situation. The discerning observer knows that there are several sides to every story, and delays forming conclusions until the situation has been thoroughly explored.

If the investigators in the popular TV series Crime Scene Investigation (CSI) were to jump to conclusions and judge a situation before exploring it, they would never capture the perpetrator. Instead, they research every shred of evidence before forming conclusions.

It is the judging that we do, instead of the discerning that we ought to do, that causes us to shut ourselves off from others. By judging, we presume our assumptions are correct. Judging keeps us isolated, whereas discernment causes us to investigate and check out our assumptions. Discernment leads to a greater possibility of connection and integration with others.

Faulty Perception

People often become resentful, not because of what someone did but because of what the other person did not do. People who are vigilant to the reactions that others have toward them are bound to be disappointed, because it is almost impossible for anyone to give us exactly what we need.

Imagine Jeff cares so much about how others react to him that he has a mental list of appropriate behaviors his co-workers should display toward him. What happens when he works with someone who focuses more on tasks than on relationships?

This task-oriented person consistently refuses to join after-work team activities. This does not fit with Jeff's expectations of how co-workers should behave. This person does not give Jeff feedback or attention unless it is relevant to the job at hand. Jeff perceives his co-worker's attention to task as rejection.

With Jeff's need to receive approval, he resents this person for rejecting him. Jeff even starts a rumor that the unresponsive co-worker is a snob. This perceived and imagined wrong is self inflicted and then projected onto someone else. No wrong was committed, yet Jeff is in danger of stewing with resentment unless he checks his perception of reality.

CHAPTER IV

COMPASSION BRINGS HAPPINESS

*H*AVE YOU EVER FELT SO DEEPLY AND CARED SO MUCH FOR OTHERS THAT YOU WISH YOU COULD TRADE PLACES WITH THEM OR CARRY SOME OF THEIR PAIN?

This Is Compassion

What mother has not seen her child in the clutches of an illness and fervently wished that the illness be transferred to her? The original meaning of the word passion is to suffer for a cause. Compassion means to suffer with another person. When one is compassionate, the soul has evolved. Compassionate people have developed a disposition toward love, mercy, and loving kindness. To inflict pain onto another person is tantamount to inflicting pain onto themselves, so finely tuned are their sensitivities.

Generally, compassion is a cultivated trait. Throughout a lifetime, we discover that compassion does not necessarily mean doing for another, but it means being with another in times of sorrow and challenge. As we develop compassion for others, we can increase compassion for ourselves. As we show compassion for ourselves, we can bestow the same gift upon others.

What Compassion Is Not

When a friend did not return my call for three weeks, I sent her an e-mail asking what was going on. She e-mailed back saying she was going through a difficult time. She was feeling grouchy, negative, and more than a little depressed. She had not called me or any of her other friends because she felt it was not fair to burden us with her troubles. Well! I felt sad for her and for me. I felt sad because she had prejudged me and I did not concur with her choice to stay in touch only when she was feeling in top form. I was frustrated because too many sayings such as *I'm cutting all negative people out of my life,* have become mantras, adopted as if they are rules written in stone. Moreover, showing up in our friends lives only when all is well is a sign of a very fragile relationship.

Compassion is not pity. To feel pity is to elevate ourselves as better than the other person. Nor is compassion a take-charge attitude where we eliminate the source of their pain. Compassion is not easy. Being with someone during a time of great turmoil may trigger our own pain. For example, what if a friend loses her father and is in the deepest pit of unimaginable grief? If you have also lost your father, the pain of his loss may come bubbling up to the surface. To stay with your friend, holding her and continuing to comfort her when you yourself are in need of comfort, requires great strength of character. It would be easy to transfer attention from her feelings of grief to your own similar feelings, but it would break your intention of providing compassion.

23

The solution is to feel rather than dismiss your own vulnerabilities while continuing to be present for your friend. To give compassion is to receive compassion. Most important is that when you give compassion, your own healing advances. To reduce your own pain by turning away from your friend is to turn away from your own healing. It is true – what we give to others returns to us on wings!

Those who grew up in any Christian faith were taught that one of the last feelings and emotions Christ had before He died was compassion. "Forgive them for they know not what they do," were among the last words He said before he died. Therefore, when we feel compassion and forgive, we are Christ-like and walking in His ways.

What must we do if we meet someone who appears to be evil? We must feel compassion for this person whose reaction to painful events has sentenced him or her to a life bereft of love, compassion, and kindness. Judgment will only injure our spirit, creativity, and peace of mind. Then it would be wise to absence ourselves from his or her presence! There is nothing to be gained by exposing ourselves to someone who has demonstrated a lack of character. Instead, trust your instinct and move away, quickly. As Maya Angelou told Oprah, "when people tell you who they are, believe them!"

Feeling compassion costs nothing, but feeling hatred costs you your peace of mind.

Some people must feel compassion for themselves before they can show compassion for others. Conversely, some people must feel compassion for others before they can feel it for themselves. Whatever your path, it is imperative you begin immediately to cultivate compassion.

Begin developing compassion by focusing on one person, perhaps someone you know fairly well. Although television commercials about third world children in need of foster parents might cause a few moments of compassion, the source of the despair is so far from our experience that true compassion soon fades. Instead, pick a familiar person who has been hurtful. Be willing to feel one percent compassion for that person today. Feel one percent compassion each time you think of that person and the unifying spirit of the universe will come running toward you to close the remaining ninety-nine percent gap.

Continue feeling compassion, one percent at a time, until you feel about sixty-five percent compassion for that person. Then pick someone else. Sixty-five percent is a critical mass. At this point, your obsessive ruminating and negative feelings will be almost non-existent. You may think of the person and the accompanying hurt occasionally, but the intensity is subtle rather than dramatic. Perfectionism, wanting to be one hundred percent free of that situation, will stop the efforts of those with the most noble of intentions. Sixty-five percent is not perfect but it is enough for now. The other thirty-five percent will work itself out in the process of life itself.

I feel compassion for anyone consumed by resentment, anger, hate, and fear, because I know from personal experience the amount of emotional energy it takes, and the physical drain that holding onto those destructive emotions can cause. I know the frown lines that appear on the faces of people held captive this way.

Some unfortunate people go through life without the ability to feel compassion for others. Deep in their hearts, there is a feeling of separation, a lack of trust. These people fear that others will not extend compassion to them. This is because they hold a deep-seated belief that whatever troubles and suffering they have endured, those troubles were brought on by themselves. Therefore, they are not deserving of comfort in times of sorrow.

Only God (or one's definition of a Higher Power) is perfect. Yet we hold on to the erroneous notion of perfectionist standards, as if to be imperfect is to sin. By the way, sin is an archery term that means to fall short of the mark, the bulls-eye. When we see others falling short of the mark, rather than seeing them as imperfect human beings just like us, we view them as flawed. Picking out faults in others is relatively easy because we are very familiar with finding fault with and judging ourselves. We all have bosses, in-laws, family, and past relationships. Scan the following list and note who (and what) causes you to feel judgmental:

- I resent my boss/ex-boss because _____
- I resent my husband/wife because _____
- I resent my ex-husband/ex-wife because _____
- I resent my mother/father because_____
- I resent my grandmother/grandfather because_____
- I resent my aunt/uncle because _____
- I resent my mother-in-law because _____
- I resent my father-in-law because _____
- I resent my boyfriend/girlfriend because_____
- I resent my ex-boyfriend/ex-girlfriend because _____
- I resent my sister/brother because_____
- I resent my sister-in-law because_____
- I resent my brother-in-law because_____
- I resent my neighbor because _____
- I resent my teacher because _____
- I resent my friend because _____
- I resent my co-worker because _____
- I resent people who are racially different because_____
- I resent people who are fitter than me because_____
- I resent those of a different sexual orientation _____

Going through this exercise is a very effective method for uncovering prejudices and judgments where we thought none existed. Awareness is the first step to change and we all know that it is impossible to have peace of mind where judgments and resentments take precedence.

CHAPTER V

DEFENSIVE BEHAVIOR

*C*HILDREN ARE THE WORLD'S GREATEST
DEFENSE EXPERTS. IN EVERY CULTURE ONE OF
THE FIRST GAMES A CHILD LEARNS TO PLAY IS
"LET'S PRETEND!"

Our imagination can protect us

Children can take a block of wood and pretend it is a fire engine. Some children prefer playing with pots and pans rather than toys.

It is not only instinctive for children to use imagination, it is necessary. How else do children build defenses to carry them through the formative, sometimes traumatic years? To a child, life can be deadly serious. Adults often forget how big and scary things can be through a child's eyes. Simple events take on the appearance of life and death. Without the ability to fantasize, there might be no way to escape the terror. The survival of the human race depends upon developing the skills of escaping into, and comforting ourselves with, creativity and play. Every childhood trauma must be equalized by a defense that allows the child to cope with that difficult situation. Imagination and the subconscious mind come to their rescue.

With no previous experience by which children can explain traumatic and scary situations to themselves, they have to choose to spend time either in fear or in fantasy. The likely result is they become mired in fear and will either become angry and defensive or passive and withdrawn. Neither of these two coping behaviors is ideal.

Since the main objective of our species is survival, threatening situations cause children to find ways to dilute or neutralize the threat. What makes children so good at this is their ability to tell themselves what to feel. They create defenses that give them the feeling of safety and well-being. They trick themselves into a frame of mind that makes everything seem okay. Even if these defenses are imaginary or irrational, the fantasy becomes real to them.

For a defense to work, a new personality, different from the one we were born with, must form. By the time we reach adulthood we have accumulated a truckload of defenses, subconsciously designed for our own protection. We created these defenses to help us cope with the far-reaching negative consequences of receiving conditional love, instead of life-affirming unconditional love.

When we reach adulthood, our future is already compromised because we are identified closely with our defenses. We consider our defenses healthy, normal, and necessary for survival. Living defensively carried us safely through our formative years., Continuing to live inside our defenses carries a harsh price.

As long as we identify with our defenses, we have no idea who it is that we are or why we are doing what we are doing. In the adult world, we are not able to be as self-reliant as we would be with no defenses and no pretenses. Sadly, most people expend a tremendous amount of energy to defend their defenses. However, those who argue for their defenses are merely arguing for their limitations!

Here is the problem facing us today. Each aspect of our personality (and we have hundreds, one to balance each trauma that we experienced as we grew up) has a different set of values. Each personality has a different set of rules to follow, a moral standard of its own and its own code of ethics. We have a personality for driving on the freeway, one for work, and one for home and family. We put on a different face for the doctor, banker, minister, traffic cop, friends, and etcetera. Each personality has its own mechanism, vocabulary, and protocol.

That is why it is difficult for us to know who we are. Waking each morning we are never certain which of these personalities is going to take charge, which one will drive the car to work. This causes problems. The biggest problem is in interpersonal relationships. Without knowing why, we may feel misunderstood, judged, and criticized. In turn, we misunderstand others. We judge them stupid, thoughtless, cruel, and so on. Our defenses are so deeply entrenched and automatic that we are unaware of them. Instead of evaluating ourselves, we make the other person wrong and let it go at that.

We all have defenses; we are aware of some of them and oblivious to others. However, wouldn't it be refreshing if we were able to acknowledge to each new person we meet, "Hello there. I am now connecting to you with my protective defenses intact, and I see that you want to connect with me with your defenses intact." Instead, we put on our social face (a.k.a. mask) and hope for the best and then become upset when he or she says or does something to disappoint us!

Is it any wonder that developing healthy relationships takes so much time and causes so much confusion? Valuable questions that each of us should ask ourselves are:

- What are my defenses?
- Which defenses serve me for my greater good?
- How much more magnificent would I be without my defenses?
- What am I going to do about the defenses that do not serve me?

When you accept the personal challenge of examining your defenses, you can decide whether to remain under their control. Once examined, you may decide to eliminate or update them. I contend that for each defense you manage to bring under control, you will multiply your freedom and personal power.

One straightforward prayer of affirmation that may help you with this process is, *God, please heal me of the limiting decisions I made in childhood that may have helped me cope then but do not serve me now.*

Put in the form of an affirmation you might repeat, *I now release myself from the decisions I made in childhood that may have served me well then but do not serve me now.*

I realize that as an adult my erroneous beliefs and defenses are my worst enemy, even though they were my best friend as a child. Like make-believe and night-lights, I must let them go. What I have learned about myself in the past from religion, teachers, philosophers, counselors, and other authorities is highly valuable. However, the truth about my core beliefs and defenses is *the truth* I have been searching for all along. This truth can set me free to be who I am; to be authentic.

Why would an adult build a wall to keep others out? Fear? Control? Habit? It makes sense that one would want to keep the enemy out, but why would one want to keep friends at a distance? A person with highly activated defenses is always on the lookout, constantly on guard for infractions. When an infraction occurs, that person's defenses rear up and attack meets attack. Distance and separation ensue. Unfortunately, for many of us this situation occurs more often than we would like.

Common Labels

When we live defensively, our feelings of importance often come at the expense of others and consequently our feelings of comfort, pleasure, and peace of mind are rare and fleeting. Instead, despite our best efforts and desires we receive negative responses from others. Paradoxically, those who judge us as unworthy of their attention also demonstrate defensive behavior. It is a classic case of the pot calling the kettle black. Some of the perceptions people have about us when we behave defensively are listed below.

Our defenses keep us in spiritual poverty. Defenses keep any supportive benefactors at a distance, outside our personal circle, and we are unable to tap into the good graces of others. Defenses keep us lonely because we keep our true selves from those we love – our children, spouse, lover, friends, and co-workers. Many of us deny we have such defenses but this may be a self-deception. Thinking I do not have defenses is itself a defense.

Common Defenses

Check this list of common defenses and determine which ones apply to you:

Accusing	Aggressive	Agreeing
Angry	Analyzing	Arguing
Attacking	Avoiding	Besmirch
Blaming	Bullying	Conforming
Defiant	Denying	Demanding
Disrespecting	Explaining	Frowning
Generalizing	Glaring	Gossiping
Grinning	Intellectualizing	Intimidating
Joking	Justifying	Judging

Labeling	Lying	Minimizing
Obedient	Pouting	Procrastinating
Uttering profanities	Protecting	Putting others down
Projecting	Questioning	Quoting scripture
Quibbling	Retaliating	Rationalizing
Shouting	Silent treatment	Sarcastic
Smug	Staring	Stealing
Superior	Theorizing	Threatening
Verbalizing	Withdrawing	Whining

Eliminating Defenses

There is no limit to our capacity to dismantle defenses. I recommend you carry a small notepad to record the defenses you would like to review. You may then do the work at a convenient time. Do not think too much about results. If you continue the process for a few months, you will find that behavioral changes are taking place without even thinking about it. Businesses conduct an ongoing inventory because knowing what they have (do not have) in stock helps them plan and make better decisions to help their business thrive while their competition that stays in denial may fail.

First, notice the defense in action. For instance, did you notice your instinct to either withdraw or attack when a partner told you something you did not want to hear? You might ask yourself some questions to help put that defense in perspective. The key to releasing a defense is to know and understand its underbelly. As an example, let us examine the thought process you might use to know and understand the underbelly of this defense.

1. Is it _good_ for me to attack/withdraw from others?
2. Is it _good_ for me to expect others not to say anything that upsets me?

3. Is it <u>bad</u> for me to attack/withdraw from others?
4. Is it <u>bad</u> for me to expect others not to say anything that upsets me?
5. Is it <u>good</u> for others to attack/withdraw from people?
6. Is it <u>good</u> for others to expect not to have anything said that will upset them?

After each of these questions ask yourself, either "What do I think about this?" or "How do I feel about this?" You can use this questioning sequence to scrutinize any concept, defense, attitude, idea, belief system, behavior, action, thought, plan or goal that you choose.

CHAPTER VI

HOW I APPEAR
TO OTHERS

*W*ITH EVERY ACTION THERE IS AN EQUAL
AND OPPOSITE REACTION. SO HOW DO YOUR
ACTIONS AND BEHAVIOR AFFECT HOW OTHERS
WILL REACT TO YOU?

Which Defenses Describe Me?

This exercise helps you understand how you, with your defenses, appear to others. Use the words listed below to complete the following activity. You may find that more than one word fits the defense you are working on. You may also think of a word not listed. Use the word that is most appropriate for you. It is important not to interpret these words or situations as wrong. They are merely guidelines to assist in creating a clearer picture. Knowing ourselves, not condemning ourselves, is the first step toward self-awareness.

When we complete this inventory and find ourselves wanting, we receive two benefits. First, we have a heightened awareness of ourselves. Second, we might reduce our tendency to criticize others and realize that to criticize others is to criticize ourselves. When we are criticized, our emotional stress increases, and our adrenal glands release cortosol in response to the stress. When we criticize others, the body reacts in exactly the same way.

We leave an impression on those around us when we use defensive behaviors.

1. When I accuse, I appear _____
2. When I am aggressive, I appear _____
3. When I analyze, I appear_____
4. When I am angry, I appear _____
5. When I argue, I appear _____
6. When I avoid, I appear _____
7. When I blame, I appear_____
8. When I complain, I appear _____
9. When I conform, I appear_____
10. When I am defiant, I appear _____
11. When I demand, I appear _____
12. When I swear and tell off-color jokes, I appear _____
13. When I am passive, I appear _____
14. When I am disrespectful, I appear_____
15. When I explain, I appear_____
16. When I frown, I appear_____
17. When I generalize, I appear_____
18. When I gossip, I appear_____
19. When I ignore, I appear _____
20. When I intellectualize, I appear_____
21. When I intimidate, I appear _____

22. When I joke _____

23. When I judge _____

24. When I justify and defend, I appear _____

25. When I label _____

26. When I lie _____

27. When I minimize _____

28. When I obey _____

29. When I procrastinate _____

30. When I use profanity _____

31. When I project _____

32. When I protect _____

33. When I put people down _____

34. When I question _____

35. When I quote scripture to make me right
    and others wrong_____

36. When I rationalize _____

37. When I retaliate _____

38. When I am sarcastic _____

39. When I shout _____

40. When I am silent _____

41. When I am smug _____

42. When I steal _____

43. When I act superior _____

44. When I theorize _____

45. When I threaten _____

46. When I verbalize _____

47. When I whine _____

48. When I withdraw _____

Choice versus Habit

Before we decide to do something against our own best interests, we usually have a brief moment of sanity. This moment is the gap between doing something self-supporting and doing something that feels good right now but will cause pain later. When we choose the path that contains long periods of challenge, our victim load lessens and our ability to be our own best agent deepens. Whenever we grasp that small moment of sanity, we become a center of benevolent power and influence over ourselves. Ultimately, our own power is the only earthly power that we can absolutely rely upon. As the number of incidents increase when we practice mastery over our fear, doubt, and insecurities, our sense of self increases and self-esteem grows naturally. I personally know of no other path to self-esteem.

When we live in fear, we suppress many emotions and attitudes. Just as an autoimmune disease attacks our own organs, joints and ligaments, not keeping our word to ourselves or to others, for whatever reason, attacks our own core identity. This self-attack occurs when we store the psychic message, *how fraudulent! I say one thing and do another. I want things out of life but do not take the appropriate action to attain or attract them. I have values but do not live by them.* The best laid plans and a commitment to positive thinking does not work if our unconscious core beliefs demand otherwise. A core belief is an unconsciously held principle that dictates our behavior, despite the conscious thoughts we have about our decisions and actions.

What we gain by suppressing our emotions is temporary relief from the symptoms of separateness. Nevertheless, the separation widens. Our relationship with others worsens and, paradoxically, so does our relationship with ourselves. In the end, relationships endure not just because of the words expressed or the feelings demonstrated but also because of the actions that are taken on a consistent basis.

When we conveniently tell a lie, make promises we do not keep, are inconsistent, or say negative things to or about others, we are seen as being untrustworthy, undependable, unaccountable, and irresponsible, even though at the time we may have fully intended to keep our promise. We could ask ourselves this question: *how do I really feel about myself when I make promises but do not keep them, or when I make excuses and do not say what I mean?*

The answer is simple, isn't it? We feel fragile and have a shaky self-concept. Our core identity is not strong. Guess what? We ought to spend as much time discovering our core identity as we do working to attain hard skills; skills that are easy to measure, such as the ability to write a new business plan, plan a family outing, develop new products, or manage a team.

The first time you react according to your new plan, take pause. Coming from choice versus habit will be a momentous occasion! There is power in your action, a power from within, coming from the mental process that created choice. Internal power comes from choosing how you behave. You will be very effective when you have achieved mastery over your own actions and reactions. You will be able to deal with life on life's terms. The biggest gift of all is that you will return to the core personality and spirit that you had when you were born.

Motivation and Passion

Many people wonder what it takes to motivate themselves, their children, or their employees. I believe that motivation is the willingness to feel the pain and to pay the necessary price to achieve our goals. Nothing, at least nothing good, comes without effort and a price. Even loving and nurturing our children, while one of life's most rewarding experiences, comes at a price as all parents will agree.

Passion is that willingness to pay the price. Passion provides the energy to keep going when everything around us is falling apart. According to the *Bloomsbury Dictionary of Word Origins*, the word passion is derived from the Latin word *pati*, which means to suffer. *Pati* is also the root of the English word *patient* which also means to suffer (those who are patient actually suffer while waiting for their desired outcome). Similarly, passive comes from the Latin word *pass* meaning capable of suffering. Aggression and passivity are two sides of the same coin. Both feelings are a fearful response to pain and suffering.

Passion will help change both those feelings into courage and action. Passion has come to mean strength of feeling. Therefore, we would expect that if passion, or strength of feeling, is strong enough, we would be willing to suffer for our visions, dreams, and goals. Fear is the root of passion; passion motivates us to courage; courage motivates us to action.

Given that we have many fears, how do we make it through the day achieving as much as we do? We do so by having great intentions, by thinking that time will heal all wounds. But time alone will not ease our pain.

When imagination provides us with desires, dreams, and goals but we do not take the necessary action, we live a fantasy life rife with magical thinking. We believe that time, distance, and luck will intervene on our behalf. A friend told me that she sings and writes twenty-five affirmations three times a day. I believe that when she is ready to take the action, to pay the price, she will move from magical thinking (affirmations) to creativity. Although there is nothing intrinsically wrong with affirming a desired goal, it cannot take the place of action, even imperfect action. Passion (fear) and action always precede creativity. We judge ourselves on what we intend to do, but the world judges us on what we actually do. And everything we want is on the other side of fear, including lots of doing, trying, failing, and succeeding.

Fear is the root of Passion

Passion motivates us to Courage

Courage motivates us to Action

Alice Wheaton ©
2005

Tyranny of the Nice

The agenda of passive-aggressive people is never to be hurt. Their feelings are close to the surface and their agenda is not to feel anything they do not want to feel.

Sadly, however, if they are in any form of relationship this agenda is impossible. Partners will inadvertently say and do (or not say or not do) things that affect their passive-aggressive sensibilities. Rather than assertively standing up for themselves, the passive-aggressive person's feelings go underground. However, they tolerate only so many infractions and then they retaliate. Instead of coming out swinging a visible stick, they carry a heavy club (albeit invisible) behind their back. They swing and hit, and the person being clobbered does not even see it coming. Nor does the person know what he or she did to deserve it. It is even possible that the punishment is for something that happened months ago! The tyranny of this scenario is that passive-aggressive people can present a demeanor of sweetness and niceness, but underneath they are just as resentful and judgmental as your average aggressive, blustery person.

Both aggressive and passive-aggressive people are controlling. People who are aggressive and confrontational are just as afraid of confrontation as people who are passive and timid. Aggressive people are so afraid of showdowns that they pre-empt them by being the type of person others are afraid to approach. Aggressive people control others by being unsafe to receive truthful feedback. If I tell you my truth and you become angry with me, I will think twice before I ever again trust you enough to tell you my truth again.

The problem with someone who practices passive aggression is only he or she knows the rules of the game. Partners are set up to fail, and fail they do, which causes the passive-aggressive partner to become even more resentful and angry. He or she then ups the ante and changes the rules. It is a difficult situation, even for the perpetrator of the game.

Personally, I unequivocally prefer the truth because then I can get a grip on the situation and respond accordingly. When someone presents an issue to me in a delicate fashion, I simply might not get it.

Recently, someone mentioned that I often do not end my sentences. He laughingly said he not only had to listen to me but he also needed to think like me. As we discussed this particular habit of mine he asked, "How did I do at finishing your sentence? I'm good at thinking like you, aren't I?"

My friend believed he had discussed his concern with me but that was not my understanding. I understood that he noticed this trait and was lovingly indulging me. I felt he was laughing with me not at me, and that he was actually quite happy with me, quirks and all.

However, the opposite was true. He was quite irritated with me, although he never once said, "You finish your statements in mid-sentence and I feel frustrated about that. My judgment is that you are treating me with disrespect. You can carry on a full conversation with your clients, but lose your train of thought when talking to me. How can we work this out?"

What I thought was understanding was actually betrayal. I felt loved, accepted, and understood, when in fact, he resented me! The unequivocal truth is never brutal. However, unequivocal resentment and the distance it creates are quite harsh. Passive aggression is a fool's game. Only the person with the invisible club knows the rules. But since any frequently played game eventually becomes boring, the rules change and the passive-aggressive person ups the ante. Passivity, like outward aggression, is just another face of fear.

The solution is for people to begin slowly to create boundaries and to tell their truth in the moment. It is impossible for someone to stand in their circle of benevolent power if they cannot create personal boundaries. Likely, they will not need to be adamantly aggressive. In moments of confusion or tension, he or she just needs to say, "Tell me what you mean," or "I feel uncomfortable when you do that and I would like you to stop." These statements made repeatedly in a quiet voice will eventually be effective. They will not work immediately because those in relationships with passive-aggressive people know very well that he or she can do or say almost anything with no direct consequences. The rule of changing one percent at a time applies here as well.

Many passive-aggressive types when confronted with, "What's wrong? What did I do now?" will say, "Nothing." This is a crazy-making moment because the words say one thing but the body language states another – tight lips, rigid posture, no eye contact, sighing, and so on. A lose-lose game is played out by two frustrated people. Passive-aggressive types are fuelled by the hidden pride they have in their seeming goodliness, in their ability to come to insights (actually judgments), and in their self-proclaimed humility and sensitivity. When people tell me they are sensitive, my radar is engaged and I wonder if they say this because of their deep sensitivity to themselves, because a heightened sensitivity to self precludes sensitivity to others.

Sometimes those sweet, timid people who are so sensitive that they must not be forced to bear the harsh burden of the truth are merely practicing tyranny of the nice.

Chapter VII

COMFORT ZONES

$\mathscr{E}$VERYONE ENJOYS THE FEELING OF BEING IN CONTROL. YOU KNOW EXACTLY WHAT IS GOING TO HAPPEN NEXT AND JUST WHAT YOU ARE GOING TO DO ABOUT IT. ROUTINE CREATES A SAFE FEELING.

Growth Lies beyond Comfort

The truth is you will not be comfortable when you first try to form new habits. You will desperately want to scurry back to your comfort zone, or rather, your familiar discomfort zone.

It is natural to feel this way – most people do. Getting out there without all the skills, even when you feel anxiety and trepidation, is easier in the end than watching those who are less competent charm the boss, get the promotion and move to the top of the pack.

After surgery, the sensation of your body healing is quite uncomfortable. Forming new habits feels like that. Everyone who tries new techniques or systems feels uncomfortable, artificial and maybe even a little manipulative until the new processes become integrated into their skill set. This is the time to be willing to live with and to manage your uncomfortable feelings.

My Comfort Zone

I used to have a comfort zone where I knew I couldn't fail,
The same four walls and busy work were really more like jail.
I longed so much to do the things I'd never done before,
But I stayed inside my comfort zone and paced the same old floor.

I said it didn't matter that I wasn't doing much,
I said I didn't care for things like diamonds, cars and such.
I claimed to be so busy with the things inside the zone,
But deep inside I kept longing for some victory of my own.

I couldn't let my life go by just watching others win,
I held my breath and stepped outside to let the change begin.
I took a step and with new strength I'd never felt before,
I kissed my comfort zone good-bye and closed and locked the door.

If you are in a comfort zone, afraid to venture out,
Remember all winners were once with similar doubt.
A step or two, a 'do it' attitude, can make your dreams come true,
Create your future with your eyes wide open; success is there for you.

—Anonymous

45

I have two wishes about this poem. The first is that I wish I had written it. Second, I wish I knew the author's name, so I could give him or her the credit that is due.

Perfectionism is a crime against success

Too often children are told they should be seen and not heard. What devastation to heap on a little heart! The message is this: *if you are not pleasing to my ears, you must be quiet. Unless what you say as a child makes sense to me, what you have to say is unworthy (and therefore you yourself are unworthy).* To a child, being worthy equates to having a beloved parent's approval.

Another saying children hear is: *if a job is worth doing, it is worth doing right.* This is also stated as: *if you're going to do it, do it right the first time.* Again, what utter nonsense! A job worth doing is worth doing over, and over, and over again. All children should be allowed, even encouraged, to do the best they can until they learn the new skill. When they are told to do it right the first time they naturally become procrastinators or perfectionists because they do not want to make a mistake and run the risk of receiving a parent's criticism.

Another misguided saying *is it is okay to make a mistake; just do not make the same one twice.* Ask any successful person and he or she will tell you that sometimes it takes several repeated mistakes to achieve success. Repeated mistakes actually get us closer to the solution…just like Thomas Edison who apparently tried 10,000 times to invent the light bulb. If we were all programmed to try only once, we would all be in the dark much longer!

The deep-seated need for perfection spills over into expecting perfection in others. Judging others negatively may become a way to express one's own deeply rooted anger toward oneself for not getting everything right the first time. What a terrible cycle to impose on our bodies, emotions, and intellect.

It is time to practice loving kindness to ourselves, to all others we have known in the past, and to those who we will meet in the future. *Show me a perfectionist and I will show you a procrastinator.* Show me a perfectionist and I will show you someone who is critical of him or herself and, therefore, critical of others.

CHAPTER VIII

FEAR IS NORMAL

*F*EAR IS A PERFECTLY NORMAL WAY TO FEEL. WITHOUT FEAR, THERE WOULD BE NO INSTINCT OF SELF-PROTECTION.

Fear Provides a Source of Comfort

Consider the wild antelope's response to fear. The fearful minority of the herd – about twenty percent – protect the more relaxed majority. When a twig snaps or the wind carries a new scent, the fearful minority runs for cover and the remaining eighty percent follow. Any members of the herd who are slow to respond are prey for the predators.

People respond similarly to danger. Our heightened senses tell us when a person or a situation is unsafe. We respond in a self-protective manner. We have fear; fear does not have us.

Unfortunately, that is where the similarity ends. Unlike antelopes, humans project into the future. With fearful thinking, they imagine catastrophic results for themselves and for those around them. This catastrophic thinking occurs without grounding in reality but our imagined disasters feel so real that they stop us from achieving our dreams, visions, and goals.

Psychologists generally agree that our first emotional response to change is fear. It is as if our ego and our subconscious mind are ganging up to convince us of unimaginable dangers. Fear convinces us that we will be worse off in the future than we are now. Since most people believe everything they think (erroneously), only the brave move ahead to where they want to be, facing the possibility that all of the imagined fears will actually come to fruition. Successful people know that lasting success comes from *failing forward.*

Most people do whatever they can to avoid coming face to face with fear. In reality, without fear there is no courage. We can move from fear to passion, passion to courage, courage to imperfect action, and imperfect action to success.

Emotional Content of Fear

Fear shows up in our lives in the form of passivity, aggression, or passion. It can take any one of these forms, or a combination of them.

Behaviors typical of FEAR		
PASSIVITY	AGGRESSION	PASSION
Submissive	Controlling Intimidating	Courageous
Distant Resentful	Frustrated	Motivated

The first column below shows behaviors you typically exhibit when ruled by fear. This is contrasted in the second column by the thoughts, beliefs, and behaviors you have when you feel love and find peace of mind. As you read the comparisons in the Peace of Mind column, consider what the benefits of enjoying this state of consciousness would be to you.

When ruled by fear:	Coming from love & peace of mind
Seeks to be understood	Accepts self and others
Makes promises but does not keep them	Gives word and keeps it
Blames others for situations, circumstances	Is kind and nurturing
Gossips	Reports only on the good of others
Can't stand to feel pain or discomfort; defends comfort zone	Is willing to face fear and be uncomfortable
Takes credit when credit is not due	Is responsible and asks "What is it about me?"
Lies, cheats, steals	Tells the truth and is honest
Justifies and defends	Is accountable
Withholds	Is generous
Is contemptuous before examination	Is open-minded to other's opinions
Is bossy	Gives choices
Is violent	Is calm and loving
Is self-centered	Can balance self-care with other-care
Is critical of self and others	Gives positive feedback easily
Is afraid to try	Is willing to fail

Controls	Demonstrates 'live and let live' attitude
Is unfaithful	Is loyal
Is addicted	Is clean and sober
Is resentful	Forgives others

Fear and Consciousness

Fear has its own consciousness. This consciousness uses food supplied by our minds, by our core beliefs, by our thinking and eventually by our actions. Thoughts of resentment and anger fuel fear; it keeps alive that which hurts us and instead of reminiscing over the good times, we fuel the very memories that cause our distress. I know that this is easier to say than to do. I also know from personal experience that while we will never forget, forgiveness does remove the distressing charge so that when we recall the betrayal and subsequent hurt the thoughts do eventually become neutral.

What does fear want of us? Fear's agenda is to keep us stuck, never experiencing personal growth. It wants us to feel small, unempowered, and unable to express creativity. We act small and let fear grow. When so many powerful fears exist in our minds, we go through our days (and our relationships with lovers, family members, and friends) contracted by fear. No wonder so many of us cannot take life on life's terms.

Somehow, we have to shield ourselves from all those fears. That is why we build defenses, one by one and ten by ten. Consequently, we are in a constant state of physical and spiritual hunger. We get by on crumbs, starving for balance and connection with others, hungry for our creativity to shine.

We need to discover our real selves, the selves we would have been had we not taken on so many fears. Imagine the lightness of being of people who manage to go through life without the limiting emotion of fear. When you can take a detached look at your fear, viewing it as just another disorder to overcome, you will be on the path to recovery, to a place where fear does not overcome you. When you persevere on this path, you will become enlightened and transformed, rising from survival into excellence.

Fear cannot stand the equality of two people standing together, shoulder to shoulder, facing life's challenges, facing down fear together as a united force. Fear establishes a hierarchical position and whispers, "You are more powerful than he is. You are more special." Fear can control one person but two people with an agenda for personal growth and transformation cause fear to quake. Fear will do anything it can to drive them apart. Fear wants us to feel fragmented and incomplete because a fragmented person has fewer defenses against fear than a whole person.

Here are some other ways that fear affects our consciousness. This list could be endless but you may find a statement or two here that here that resonates.

What does fear want of us?

- Fear wants us to stand alone, not to ask for help.
- Fear wants us not to recognize it for what it is.
- Fear shows many faces – arrogance, pride, and rationalization – to keep us confused and distracted.
- Fear focuses on the negative aspects of our past. It does not allow us to see the higher story behind everything we experience. Its interest is in the lower story which builds our defenses.
- Fear delivers its message through people who are sweet-sounding and solicitous. They say comforting words like, "Trust me," or

"Everyone else is doing this," and "You are more special than the others."

- Fear sends us people who say, "I only want what is good for you," or "I know what is best for you," or "You must believe what I believe to be true."
- Fear wants us to dominate others, or for others to dominate us.
- Fear wants us to take no chances. If we do take a chance we have only one chance to succeed. We must not fail and have the audacity to try again.
- Fear wants us to take critical feedback personally as evidence of our unworthiness.
- Fear wants us to compare our insides with other people's outsides.
- Fear wants us to stay in our comfort zones.
- Fear wants us to be negative thinkers. It puts ideas in our heads that seem perfectly logical and rational.
- Fear wants us to express no creativity. It wants us to believe what we have to offer is not good enough.
- Fear wants us not to believe we made a mistake. Instead, it wants us to believe we are a mistake.
- Fear wants us to be dependent on substances.
- Fear wants us to curtain off all dark aspects of ourselves. It wants us to believe we are only half acceptable.
- Fear wants us to defer to authority. It wants us not to think for ourselves.
- Fear wants us to be poor in spirit and poor in our purses.
- Fear wants us to blame others for our lowered sense of self.
- Fear wants us to be defensive, to justify and make excuses for our doing, or not doing, something.
- Fear wants us to steal the spirit of others by being intimidating, controlling, or critical.

- Fear wants us never to feel compassion and forgiveness. It wants us to live with an attitude of resentment and retribution.
- Fear does not allow us to confront those who abuse, malign, overwork, or disrespect us.

Stories That Fear Tells Us

Fear tells us stories to bring us down to size. It causes us to think of scenarios and catastrophic consequences that are out of proportion to the challenges we face. Some of these stories are listed below:

What story does fear tell you?

- If you try and fail, you will not be acceptable.
- Everyone is watching and judging you harshly.
- You are too fat, too skinny, too tall, and too short.
- No one loves you because you are unlovable.
- You do not have a right to ask for what you want.
- You deserve this beating.
- You are required to do for others what they can do for themselves.
- There is no one out there for you. You are destined to live alone forever.
- There is enough in the world for everyone else, but not for you.
- You will always be poor. You are not capable of achieving wealth.
- Everyone else is more worthy than you are.
- Greatness is for others.
- Don't dream because you cannot possibly achieve it.
- Stop believing in yourself since no one else believes in you.

- Your ideas are too far fetched to ever become a reality.
- People are making fun of you behind your back.
- That attractive person will never go out with you.
- Face it, you just don't measure up.

Fear Creates an Illusion

Fear is not real. Fear is an illusion, a thinking process that has become such a strong force in our lives that we check with it before proceeding. If that were not bad enough, we believe the advice we receive in return!

Me: Hello, fear. I'm thinking of taking a new course on earning and investing money.

Fear: What's the matter with you? All you need to do is hunker down and be more disciplined.

Me: No, I really think my approach to this topic is something to look at.

Fear: It's just a moneymaking scheme. You will take money out of your piggy bank and put it into theirs.

Me: I'd like to think bigger. I'd like to know what I want. I'd like to declare myself in the game. I feel I hold myself back and I want to change that.

Fear: How will you manage change? Who will be your friends? You are different enough from your family as it is. And time! Where will you get the time?

Me: This is my life. I know from experience that the universe will not give me anything I cannot handle. Therefore, if I cannot handle a better life, the universe will not give it to me. However, I plan to do whatever I need to do so I can handle it. You, fear, do not have a say in this. But thank you for sharing; because now I am more familiar with your voice than if you had not tried to reason with me.

Fear is seductive and cunning. Fear is baffling and powerful. Fear tells us to stop just before we get to the miracle. If we stop, fear claims a bit of our spirit. Fear whispers, "This is too hard. It shouldn't be this hard!" When we judge others, or criticize them in our minds, fear tells us we are discerning and selective. When we gossip it is fear saying, "Go ahead. It is okay to help yourself feel better by making others smaller."

Fear makes victims of us all. But when we begin an investigation into fear's purpose, power, and the techniques and ploys fear uses, fear becomes the pursued and we become the pursuers. Fear is on the ropes but retaliates by turning up the volume. It finally releases its hold when we refuse to embrace fear. We can make friends with fear. We can have conversations with fear, doing as Eleanor Roosevelt said, "Invite fear in for tea. One sugar or two? Cream? Do stay awhile. I would like to know just who you are."

When it comes to our personal growth, fear saves us when it tells us, "Do not go there." When that happens, know that is exactly where we need to go. By going there repeatedly, we increase our capacity. Our lives expand. We have a chance at the love, health, prosperity, and spirit our heart desires. We could say, "Hello, fear. You have saved me. You are my hero and I love you."

Fear does not tell us the truth, in that; our growth, passion, and purpose are exactly at the point where chaos and order meet. Every time we make the safe, no risk of failure choice, we reinforce fear. Our spirit becomes smaller and smaller. We soon avoid activities and experiences that make us feel uncomfortable. We forget that discomfort is the doorway to growth. As I said earlier, *successful people fail forward.*

As we grow, we challenge fear and our spirit grows bigger. Fear's agenda is never to be discovered. We think fear is our enemy but, in fact, fear lives in fear of being found out. Fear is terrified of our taking it on, which is why a situation usually gets worse before it gets better. Fear digs in its heels and counts on us to run back to our comfort zone. Fear wants us to feel comfortable with anger, rage, and resentment because these feelings keep us from grace and fulfillment.

The more we experience grace and fulfillment in our life, the less room there is for fear. When we wade through the quagmire of fear, we develop courage. Courage, even in the presence of fear, is perfect action because we are developing our courage. And courage, not competence, is the answer. Without fear, there is no courage.

Chapter IX

CALM YOUR FEARS

*W*HEN CONTEMPLATING A NEW SITUATION, A CHANGE, OR THE BEHAVIOR OF ANOTHER PERSON, YOU CAN TELL WHEN FEAR IS REALLY OPERATING BECAUSE FEAR SAYS THERE IS ONLY ONE OPTION: A NEGATIVE OPTION!

Release Fear and Return to Love

People who feel fear, but are not owned by it, consider the negative consequences as well as a wide range of other possibilities.

You can have fear instead of fear having you. By providing yourself with several options for the challenge you are about to face, you can calm your fearful emotions long enough for your innate voice of reason to surface.

After working with thousands of people over more than ten years, what I know for sure is that men are no more confident than women, and vice versa. C.E.O.'s have fears, doubts, and insecurities the same as front-line workers. Most people have at least three work-related problems and three personal problems causing stress and chaos in their lives at any given time.

Fear, doubt, and insecurity are natural emotions we feel in response to stress and challenges. People tell me their life-long secret is constantly feeling a certain amount of fear, doubt, and insecurity. They are under the impression they are unique in this and somehow flawed. They feel the constant presence of these emotions is evidence of low self-esteem and low self-confidence. They do not know these three emotions, to a greater or lesser degree, are constant in everyone's life.

There is one significant difference in the coping skills of high performers. High performers have a greater tolerance for fear, doubt, and insecurity. When they feel those emotions, they dig deep, drawing from their accumulated resources instead of becoming overwhelmed and giving up. They begin active problem solving.

Taking chances, making mistakes and failing is tolerable to high performers. They know it is virtually impossible to succeed without taking chances. They do not like to fail, no one does. But – and this is a big difference – they are willing to fail in pursuit of their goals.

Not making a mistake is the main agenda of those who struggle to survive and of those who fear failure. They do not like to take chances. Five main fears seem to plague most people, stopping them from having the life they dream about.

The 5 Big Fears

1. Fear of Rejection
2. Fear of Self-Promotion
3. Fear of Failure

4. Fear of Personal Greatness
5. Fear of Confrontation

Here are some questions to ask yourself when you want to take a chance but fear shows up as self-doubt and insecurity. Become an observer and name the emotion/feeling:

- Have I had this before?
- What worked then?
- How does this serve me?
- How much attention have I given this state?
- What other options do I have?
- What are my thoughts?
- How long will this fearful episode last?
- What simple changes can I make now?
- Have I asked for help or is this my secret?
- If not now, when?

1. Fear of Rejection

During one of my presentations at conferences, I ask one question very early in the program, "What is the fear that permeates most of your life?" The most common answer is fear of rejection. This response comes not only from front-line workers but also from executives. Everyone suffers from this fear – educated as well as illiterate, rich and poor, happy and unhappy, young and old, movie stars and waiters, the successful and the still struggling. This fear is the great equalizer.

Although rejection is the number one fear people struggle to master every day, I believe that fear of rejection is perfectly normal. Without it, we would not have manners and social sensibilities that allow us to be accepted into our social groupings. Imagine a clan of cave dwellers evicting one of its members. That rejected clan member probably would not survive. Without a fear of rejection, which in that time included fear of not surviving, that member might not have contributed to the well-being of the clan.

Most people believe that because they have this fear, they are insecure and lack confidence. Nothing could be further from the truth. Fear of rejection is part of our natural socialization process. Social manners and graces function to keep us established in our families, communities, and social groups.

Rejection is imminent when an individual too frequently breaks the social rules of a group. In the social order of most groups, only after the individual has consistently supported the system will the system support the individual. For those individuals who dance to the beat of a different drum, meeting their own need for autonomy and meeting the needs of the clan can be confusing and frustrating. Observing the angst that adolescents and teenagers go through to achieve this balance provides a first-hand view of the phenomenon.

A simple but difficult answer to overcoming fear of rejection is this: Be willing to be rejected.

None of us was brought into the world with an agreement in our back pocket stating, "This child will be able to go through life without ever experiencing rejection." Fear of rejection is all about the future. We speculate about the dire consequences that will happen if we receive a 'no' to our request, or if we obtain some evidence that we are not wanted on the team. But why do we think that to feel good about ourselves we have to receive only 'yes' answers? Our chances of success will increase exponentially if we are willing to receive a 'no'.

Most salespeople face fear of rejection on a daily basis. Assume that each salesperson for an office furniture manufacturing company begins the New Year with 150 accounts he or she would like to open by year-end. The salesperson that is willing to be rejected by all 150 prospects will have more success than those salespeople who avoid rejection. The salespeople who are willing to do what is required, and are willing to be rejected in the process, will almost certainly succeed. Imagine the success all salespeople would have if they endorsed a statement saying, "Yes, I am willing make the contact even if he or she rejects me." The answer is always 'NO' if you don't ask!

It is futile to tell people, *you shouldn't take rejection personally*, or *get over it* because this fear is part of our biology. We all have that gland that makes us feel fear when faced with the prospect of doing something uncomfortable or facing danger, either real or imagined. Change, even if that change will have a positive impact on our lives, will cause us to run to the comfort zone. We cannot help it. The fear center of our brain is the *amygdala*. It has been hard-wired to cause us to fear rejection and we cannot change that. However, we have the mental and emotional power to minimize its impact and therefore master its debilitating effects. We can take an oppositional approach by saying, "Fear of rejection, you may reside in me but you will never dominate me. You will not prevent me from searching out new opportunities, from playing a bigger game in life and in work."

By taking this approach, you have fear but it does not have you. Just like the other fears we deal with, fear of rejection would have us think of only one scenario, a scenario that is negative, failure-ridden, and catastrophic. Fear of rejection causes us to have terrible catastrophic thoughts about the future and to believe we will be worse off than we are now.

James is at a lively house party. There is great conversation in every corner of the living room and people are dancing to his favorite tunes on the patio. He notices a woman chatting to a group of friends and wonders if she would like to join him for a dance. As soon as he thinks of asking her, he has a parallel thought, "Are you nuts? She will say no. Everyone will be looking at you, thinking what a loser you are, and you will feel stupid."

His mouth goes dry, his heart races, and his hands become clammy just thinking about the devastating feelings he will have if he is rejected. Like a wild antelope running away when a twig snaps, his self-protection is activated. By not asking for a dance he removes himself from the source of the uncomfortable feelings. He also removes himself from potentially meeting the love of his life!

Without testing his assumptions, James made some decisions about the outcome. But here are some other possible responses from the woman with whom he wanted to dance, responses that he failed to consider:

1. Yes, I would love to dance with you.
2. I am visiting with someone I've not seen for a while. Can we dance later?
3. Sorry, I do not dance. I have two left feet. Nevertheless, I would love to chat and get to know you.
4. No, thanks. I am here with my boyfriend.
5. Thanks for asking. I do not want to dance but my friend probably will. (Then he has a referral!)

By giving himself at least five possible outcomes (see model below), *and assuring himself that neither would kill him,* he develops an experience of himself as brave and courageous instead of scared and passive.

Name It, Claim It, and Release It

Separating our actions from the fearful thoughts about our next decision will help us <u>release</u> and <u>move away</u> from being controlled by them.

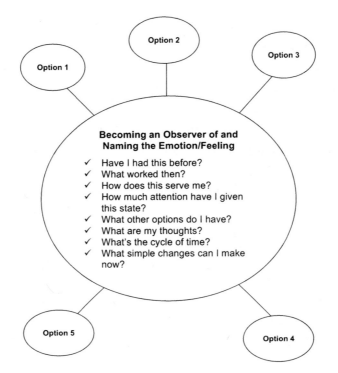

We can overcome fear of rejection by providing the opportunity for the other person to say 'no'. In fact, this increases their receptivity to saying 'yes'. A no is halfway to a yes. Next time James is at a party and is interested in dancing with a woman he could say, "Hello. You have a beautiful smile. I have been observing you for a while and I would like to ask you to dance and *feel free to say no if this doesn't work for you."* In taking this approach, he will achieve a double win. First, he takes another step in overcoming his fear of rejection and second, he has at least a fifty percent chance of connecting with a dance partner. He has given himself the opportunity to test his assumptions, not simply believing what fear was causing him to think and feel. In addition, by giving that person advance permission to say no, he held back a lot of his power whatever the outcome of his request.

Just because we think powerful thoughts and have powerful feelings, does not mean they are true. Our words are our words, our thoughts are our thoughts and our feelings are our feelings, but our actions are our life! Fear of rejection is really about the fear that if we are rejected we will not be able to manage our emotions and feelings. The good news is we can overcome this fear in a very short time. When you ask something of another person, give permission to say 'no'. You will soon begin receiving at least eighty percent of what you ask for. You will always hope for acceptance of your requests but you will not be controlled by fear, only doing that which you know will meet approval. We miss most of life by resisting rejection. Once we embrace the possibility of rejection, the universe's abundant health, prosperity, and love begins flowing toward us.

2. Fear of Self Promotion

Fear of self-promotion is complex. It includes the attitude many of us have that it is somehow wrong to put our needs and wants out front with an expectation they will be met. In a workshop called *Freeing Your Fears, Finding Your Passion*, I like to ask participants how they would describe someone who is good at self-promotion. The descriptions are generally less than favorable. Self-promoters are described as braggarts, shifty, insincere, arrogant, and pushy.

A stunned silence is usually followed by nods of recognition when I point out that people who are good at self-promotion show up for their life with passion and enthusiasm and are willing to be judged by others. Are you holding yourself back because you are trying to manage the possible future negative opinion of others? Is that another fear for you to dismantle? Do you care too much about how others will perceive you? I recently heard a saying that had a great deal of impact on me: what others think of me is none of my business! Besides, the majority of people are caught up in their own lives; they have no time or attention to pay to yours. Therefore, being convinced that we are inciting disapproval in others has a high probability of being an illusion!

Self-promoters ask for what they want and risk the rejection and judgment of others. The ingrained attitude we have – that it is not nice to show up in life bigger than we feel or to ask directly for what we want – can be transformed using three simple steps.

Three elegant steps to ask for what you want:

Step #1: Give them Permission to Say No to You: this confused your fear invite the other person the right to say no. For example, "What I'd like to do, if it's alright with you..."

Step #2: Ask Three Times before Giving Up
Be willing to ask three times. We miss one hundred percent of what we do not ask for. If we do not ask, the answer is always no!

Step #3: Be Willing to Feel as if You are being Judged/Looking Foolish
Be willing to be judged by those more fearful than you!

3. Fear of Failure

Most parents will not allow a child to swear. However, our own parents repeated slogans that were much worse than the swear words they forbade us to say. "Children should be seen and not heard. If you're going to do it, do it right the first time. A job worth doing is worth doing well." These slogans, meant to inspire us to try harder, had the opposite effect. As children we knew that we could not possibly do the job right the first time, so many of us did not even try.

The two main program types that we operate from are the Mastery Program and the Perfection Program. People operating with a Mastery Program are willing to make mistakes and believe that mistakes are an important ingredient in their success. For them to learn, undertake, or implement a new process, they do not need everything to be perfect. Individuals who practice a Mastery Program do have difficult times but when a difficult situation arises, they draw upon information and resources.

Remember the character Peter Falk played in the television police drama Colombo? His character consistently implemented a system of apparent ineptitude, "But I still don't understand. Could you please explain to me one more time, if X is like this and Y is like that, then how could Z occur?" Colombo's ineptitude was a well-disguised Mastery Program.

Those who focus on developing Mastery are quick to ask for help and they are willing to admit when they do not know the answer. They do not feel shame for their lack of knowledge. They are likely to help struggling co-workers. They do not judge others but rather, offer assistance and guidance. Most importantly, they believe they can find a solution or the required lesson if they make mistake.

Perfection (fear) Model

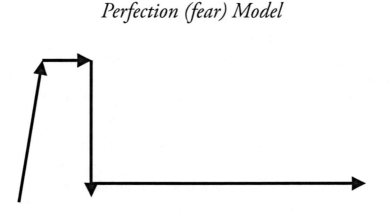

Some people who take a chance and experience failure will not be able to deal with the disappointment so will return to their comfort zone.

Success (courage) Model

Competence and self-confidence that grows and grows.

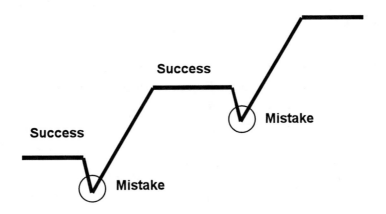

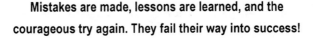

**Mistakes are made, lessons are learned, and the
courageous try again. They fail their way into success!**

Some of the people who operate with the Perfection Program, model (A) believe *they* are the mistake. Since perfectionists are unforgiving and overly critical of themselves, they tend to be less flexible and less tolerant of others. People operating in this mode need to learn to let go, one percent at a time.

Individuals who live by a Mastery Program easily out-perform those with a Perfection Program because they are willing to begin with less than 100% knowledge, skills, or attitude. I often look back on a skill or expertise I have developed, and realize that I stepped into a challenge while not knowing exactly how I would accomplish that challenge. But doing my best, and then testing and modifying along the way, helped me become more competent than I would have been if I had never taken that first step. I may never achieve excellence in most of my purists but if not, it will not be because of not taking that first step and then the next, and so on. in fact, I often laughingly tell my friends and clients that *fear, doubt, and insecurity are my three best friends!*

Both illustrations show the predictable success curve of each operating system. The diagram above shows the results people operating with a Perfection Program can expect if they are waiting to become self-confident before they make the next bold move. ***Confidence before competence is impossible.*** The result is that many of these people live in quiet desperation, stuck in hope, magical thinking, and fear. A great idea may have been born but because perfectionists don't have all the facts about the future they cannot or will not try with what they do know.

They become caught up in analysis paralysis, hoping someone will show up and observe their brilliance. They may see others, less educated but operating from a Mastery Program (on the previous page), actually succeeding. The result of this injustice makes the Perfectionist see the world as an unfair place where people who do not strive for perfection are more handsomely rewarded. They gather thoughts of resentment and blame as comfort, but they do not risk either failure or rejection.

Perfectionist thinking sounds something like this, "I can't because...," or, "I should but...," or, "What if...?" When we allow doubts to dictate our thoughts, we find ourselves in a state of *analysis paralysis.* Perfectionists prefer to do things they already do well. They avoid attempting other tasks that might challenge their knowledge and skill level, or cause them to make a mistake. Perpetual self-doubt encourages them to dwell on what they did poorly and beat themselves up for being imperfect. In other words, perfectionists disrespect themselves for being perfectly human!

Self-confidence that develops as competence increases, is lasting, and can withstand the natural ups and downs of life. Those who practice a Mastery Program of living begin with an idea, a vision, and one percent ability, knowing that expertise will develop along the way. As they make mistakes, they look for ways to learn from the situation and to increase their performance when they try again.

Whenever you tell yourself you *should* be doing something, you are actually attempting to browbeat yourself into a higher level of performance and perfectionism. A successful person knows that providing others with choice can secure agreement to move forward. Why do these perfectionists fail to recognize their own need for choice, and instead, continue to chastise themselves with the word 'should'?

When faced with a new challenge, people experience a number of self-doubt questions. Here are some of the most common:

- What if she says no to me?
- What if I feel scared or nervous?
- What if he asks me a question and I don't know the answer?
- What if I look foolish?

'What-if' questions tend to paralyze the self-doubters. They become victims of their own design. When we ask ourselves what-if questions, we are actually being self-centered. If we ask these questions of others, we can become other-centered. The old saying, "No one cares how much you know until they know how much you care," applies to everyone we meet. Asking relevant questions is an easy way to show that you care. If you are to understand someone else's needs and desires, begin the majority of your questions with the words, "What about...?" and "Tell me more..." This will cause others to feel valued and, in turn, they will be more receptive to you. Critical and judgmental self-analysis leads to self-doubt and self-defeating behaviors, in turn causing analysis paralysis.

The question that can release analysis paralysis is, "So what?" You may not have all the answers, but you can learn from your experiences and build an arsenal of information for future use. You now have more information and can try again, regardless of your earlier doubt or error. Just as a farmer harvests his crops for profit, we can harvest our weaknesses. Initially it is painful to face our dark side – to view our weaknesses and fears with compassion, as a source of personal growth – but as the strength diagram illustrates, our potential lies in actively transforming weaknesses.

By the time we are in our late 20s and 30s, we have tapped into our strengths for most of our achievements. What few people realize is that our weaknesses are also a source of potential strength and success. Successful people monitor their progress and change as needed. For example, they might hire an assistant, teach what they know, and double or even quadruple their success. They regularly tap into the power of a little-known secret: fears and weaknesses, when confronted, can be converted into strengths.

Unacknowledged weaknesses can, and will, sabotage even the best of intentions. Early success is achieved by drawing upon our strengths. Continued success depends upon building a bridge of unity between our strengths and weaknesses. When a weakness is identified and a plan of action is consistently implemented, a new strength emerges. Successful people are quite familiar with this process. They know that anything worth having is going to cause a certain amount of pain. To think otherwise is to be naive.

4. Fear of Personal Greatness

The fear of personal greatness is the most difficult of all for me to explain. Marianne Williamson, however, found no such limitation. The following excerpt from her book, *A Return to Love*, presents an explanation of this fear much more eloquently that I ever could.

> *Our deepest fear is not that we are inadequate. Our deepest fear is that we are powerful beyond measure. It is our light, not our darkness, that most frightens us. We ask ourselves: Who am I to be brilliant, gorgeous, talented and fabulous? Actually, who are*

you not to be? You are a child of God. Your playing small does not serve the world. There is nothing enlightened about shrinking so that other people won't feel insecure around you. We are all meant to shine, as children do. We were born to make manifest the glory of God that is within us. It's not in just some of us, it's in everyone. And, as we let our own light shine we unconsciously give other people permission to do the same. As we're liberated from our own fear, our presence automatically liberates others.

How to get in touch and activate your personal greatness:

1. Show up bigger than you feel.
2. Be willing to ask directly for what you want.
3. Give others the right to say no to you.
4. Improve one percent at a time.
5. Begin to give up resentment.
6. Embrace weaknesses, because once transformed they will become your strengths.
7. Ask for help.
8. Be willing to fail and try again.
9. Be willing to be rejected.
10. Do not judge your insides by other people's outsides.
11. Do not believe everything that you think.
12. Test your assumptions.
13. Offer help to others.
14. Forgive early and often.

Consider other tips for entering into your own personal greatness. What would you do today if you could jump with courage? I asked Simone, a woman in a workshop, this question and she said she would return to university to earn an MBA but she could not, because she has a full-time job and cannot afford to be a student. My question back to her was, "If not now, when?" Six weeks later she told me she had registered for two night courses. Her motivation will fuel her passion and that will help her pay the price of working and going to school. Her quest for personal greatness was hindered by the all-or-nothing approach to life. There is always a price to be paid for achieving greatness and this price can be more easily paid over time in bite-size increments. In Simone's case, two courses a semester over four years will earn her an MBA. If she waited until the time was right, in four years she'd be no further ahead.

As Marianne Williamson says, personal greatness is not in some of us; it is in all of us. I was not a writer until ten years ago when a friend gave me a book called *The Artist's Way* by Julia Cameron. The book consists of a twelve-week writing program that assists in overcoming the blocks you have, so that you can develop your artistic talent, whatever that talent may be. I have been writing and publishing ever since. To date I have published three books. I have six others in first draft and twelve booklets in production. The potential was there all along but it took Cameron's book to unlock my passion for writing.

You probably have your own personal greatness yet to be explored. Stay open and expose yourself to a variety of experiences, especially those that challenge your sensibilities. As I said in the introduction to this book, a heart that is filled with resentment, anger and fear puts up roadblocks between you and your desired life. In addition, it blocks opportunities from coming to you.

5. Fear of Confrontation

Those who fear confrontation usually have a great deal of resentment. This is because expressing boundaries or protecting themselves verbally is often very difficult, if not impossible, from their perspective. We also have trouble telling our truth in an elegant fashion. Avoiding telling another person the truth, or telling that truth in a non-supportive manner, is often the reason we need to forgive others, or to be forgiven ourselves.

It is not only what is said that hurts, but what is left unsaid. Much pain has been caused because someone with something difficult to share did not trust his or her ability to deal with the other person's reaction. The fear of confrontation was so great that the first person became convinced the other person would react badly, and so did not speak the truth – although, the other person may have reacted in a reasonable manner. Alternatively, the first person may create a situation which causes the truth to be exposed in a hurtful manner.

For example, imagine a couple that has been married for some time. One of the partners begins to feel misunderstood and undervalued, eventually leading to disinterest in the other partner. The misunderstood partner believes that sharing these feelings will make life at home uncomfortable. Fear of confrontation causes the sufferer to remain silent. Instead, the misunderstood partner has an affair. Then all hell breaks loose and the truth is finally explored. This kind of scenario is for the lucky ones. The unlucky ones continue for a lifetime with the truth left unsaid.

To be able to face our own truths we need to be able to receive feedback without detaching or becoming emotionally hooked. This also works in reverse – if we squelch our own truth, we squelch the truth of others as well.

Our personal power grows as we accept feedback without justifying or defending. When attack meets attack, fear increases for each person in the encounter. Instead of attack, you can stand in your own circle of benevolent power and say the eight magic words, "You may have a point. Tell me more."

The benefits are, first, you will have the power of self-containment instead of the darkness of control that comes from anger or withdrawal. Second, you will pave the way for communication. Your open mind and receptive behavior may open the door for vital issues to be resolved. Third, it is always important to hear what others have to say to and about you.

Ask yourself, "Is there any seed of truth in what he or she is telling me?" If there is, you can own it and change it.

By considering this possibility, you demonstrate inner strength to yourself and others. Your self-esteem will grow. Eventually you will love yourself enough that you are willing to be misunderstood by others. You will live with largess. If not now, when?

If you are waiting for everything to be just right, then life will pass you by. Are you one of those that Neil Diamond sings about in his song, *On the Way to the Sky?*

> I pity the poor one
> The shy and unsure one
> Who wanted it perfect
> But waited too long

I believe that the universe is organized around action. It obliges your subconscious craving for peace of mind by giving you opportunities to accept and work through your fear of confrontation.

Trying to understand your feelings of trepidation and unease, as if they were negative traits needing to be whipped into shape, is about as futile as pleading for stampeding horses to return to the barn. The best you can do is to accept the uncomfortable feelings, make a place for them, and tell the truth anyway. Instead of striving for understanding, it is more productive to practice acceptance of your feelings of unease by noticing what is so, without becoming emotionally hooked or making judgments that may not be accurate. Too often, someone feeling anxious and upset by a confrontation projects the responsibility for these feelings onto someone else. "You made me ..." is the blameful cry.

Practicing acceptance is to say, "This is my feeling. This is my issue. What is it about me that avoids these uncomfortable feelings at all costs?

Why do I organize my life and my relationships just to avoid being agitated?"

Organizing life, relationships, and career so as never to have uncomfortable feelings is to be dominated by fear. You miss your own power and the rewards of life. Moreover, your higher self, craving to be actualized asks, "How can I have peace if I let fear of confrontation dominate me?"

Enough is enough. Maybe age catches up with us and we change. Maybe one more loss is one too many. Maybe someone kindly declares the emperor has no clothes – the people we have co-opted into our game finally pull the plug and all hell breaks loose. Perhaps we have a 'stack attack' where our stuffed-down rage finally erupts.

Dealing honestly with that rage can lead to resolution of past issues. When that happens, the gift of peace is at our fingertips.

Over the first few months of practice, the gifts that come as a result of learning a new communication process (or, in reality, unlearning a passive style of communicating), are vast and beyond imagination. Some of these gifts include becoming known for who you truly are, being able to set and maintain boundaries, and being able to ask clearly for what you want. By anyone's standards, these are great qualities!

How does one finally expose all the desires, grief, resentment, and anger stuffed inside, layer upon layer, until there is no room for even one more issue or emotion? How does one cope when the stack finally blows, when submission, silence, depression, and illness no longer work?

In his book *Healing Back Pain*, Dr. John Sarno states that patients in his orthopaedic practice, victims of back injury, often baffled him by complaining of severe back pain long after the injury had healed. He developed the belief that our subconscious minds store issues too dark for our conscious minds to deal with, placing them out of sight in the most vulnerable parts of our body, such as an old injury.

He recommends an ongoing, deliberate conversation with our subconscious mind, even during pain-free periods. This idea made sense to me, so I created another leap of logic. We were small children when the section of our subconscious mind that harbors our limiting fears was developed. However, that section of our subconscious mind does not know we have grown up and can deal with our own truth and the truth of others, no matter how it is presented.

Imagine a father who, to emphasize a point, chastised his son by harshly poking his fingers in his young boy's chest whenever the child said something the father did not want to hear. The father might never have beaten the boy but he did no less damage because the ever-present threat was just as bad as or worse than a beating. The terrorized little boy was pushed against the wall, harder and harder.

To cope, the little boy's subconscious mind made three decisions. The first decision was always to speak kindly, not harshly, to be supportive, and to encourage niceness. "Let's all get along and not upset each other," was the unspoken agreement he entered into with those close to him.

The second decision made by his subconscious mind was never to repeat the behavior of his father. The third decision he subconsciously made was to avoid, at all costs, the overwhelming feeling of powerlessness that comes from being confronted. "I will be nice, I will not confront others, and I will not allow others to confront me."

The little boy, now an adult, continues to perpetuate the mass agreement – *you don't call me on my stuff, and I won't call you on yours.* The unfortunate result is the fear of confrontation is nurtured, while truth is denied. Is it any wonder so many people are addicted to food, smoking, drugs, alcohol, and myriad other activities and substances? Something has to compensate for all that suppression.

In Dr. Sarno's opinion, back pain is one of the prices North Americans pay for suppressing their truth and maintaining their fear of confrontation.

CHAPTER X

TELLING THE TRUTH

*I*T IS DIFFICULT TO TELL A PERSON IN
A POSITION OF AUTHORITY AND POWER OUR
TRUTH, AND YET THE TRUTH IS BEST TO BE
TOLD.

Speak with Sincerity

It is especially difficult to tell the truth to our bosses or other people whom we perceive to be a person in power. Not telling the truth reveals much about us. Our actions, not our words, show whether our values are really values or simply notions. Only in difficult times is our character revealed.

One of the ways we build character on a day-to-day basis is by facing stress and difficult issues elegantly. Some people are extremely good at telling their truth at home where they are emotionally safe, but they become timid when assertiveness is required at work, with people in power. Conversely, some powerful people at work become intimidated in their domestic partnerships. For instance, having a co-worker or boss become upset may be uncomfortable but bearable. Conversely, having a loved one become upset may be unbearable. Some people resist confrontation at all costs. They avoid any situation where there is a risk that their emotions will be hooked.

Many of us grew up hearing the Lord's Prayer in the New Testament. About halfway through it states, "Forgive us our trespasses, as we forgive those who trespass against us." I have changed this passage to, "Forgive me my trespasses, as I forgive those who trespass against me." This helps me stay humble and take responsibility in the perpetual circle of life's mistakes, forgiveness, and redemption.

I believe we should be on the lookout for reasons to forgive and opportunities to sincerely as for forgiveness. Too many people are afraid of making mistakes. Consequently, they do not take chances or stand up for themselves. As a society, we are burdened by the fear of confrontation, so much so that we tolerate the intolerable and accept the unacceptable.

The Gift of Clear Communication

To be understood and accepted is the greatest gift of all. These attributes are of great value. Whatever the relationship, the stars align and luck is on our side when understanding and acceptance are freely given as gifts.

As life would have it, achieving this state of understanding and acceptance is a convoluted, complicated undertaking, one that we rarely experience. As human beings, we strive to be understood before offering acceptance to others. But if understanding is what we crave, acceptance may never be achieved. Most issues in a relationship trigger emotions and who can explain emotions? Sometimes they are logical and understandable but more often they are not. It seems that the emotional life is lived subconsciously, arousing a conscious reaction but without a firm understanding of the cause. We think we make our decisions from logic and reason, but more likely we make them based on subconscious emotions.

We then justify those decisions with logic and reason conveniently sourced from the conscious mind. It is as if our subconscious runs the show and our conscious mind covers up for it.

When we make an effort to tell others our truth, we may experience negative consequences. Our subconscious mind reasons that someone has to pay. Most people justify and defend themselves, transferring their own frustrated feelings onto the other person through the blame game. Shame and blame come from our fear-based subconscious. The expectation is our partners and friends must know all the answers, and that with us they must conduct themselves correctly, every time. This is a need for safety. We think safety is a life without anxiety or tension. If our sensibilities are ruffled, we feel uncomfortable and we become offended.

Sometimes we wrestle a relationship into a passive state where anxiety and tension are never felt. The participants proudly proclaim, "We never disagree or fight over anything!" If they were really to tell the truth, they would also say, "And we have no juiciness, no constant learning, no pushing each other to be greater, and no spontaneous passion."

The cost of niceness is too high! All life is bipolar, constantly unfolding in a balance of peace and war, turmoil and calm, good and bad, sunset and sunrise. How naive for humans to presume that we can work, live, and play closely together without having our emotional freshness and peacefulness interrupted with periods of emotional unrest.

No one is at fault for having this desire to experience constant calm. It seems to be a natural human state, as if we were all born this way. However, we can alter our child-like expectations of an unruffled life and increase our ability to deal with a wider range of truthful communication, without feeling defensive and self-protective. We can learn to have our emotional well-being independent from the communication style of others. This deep need never to have our sensibilities affected, or our feathers ruffled as the old saying goes, is quite controlling. We are so intent not to have those sensibilities affected that we enter into a social agreement, *You don't call me on my stuff, and I won't call you on yours.* This mass consciousness of denying our truth, which masquerades as civility, is really a malignant niceness.

Those who buy into *niceness at all costs* lead lives of quiet desperation. The absence of evident pain is countered by the absence of intense pleasure. There is neither friction nor passion, neither confrontation nor truth. What does exist is a truce, but a truce does not lead to peace of mind – a wild peace that can burst into an erotic bath or a fantasy fulfilling Saturday afternoon. Molding one's truth so as not to trigger another's fear of confrontation is disloyal to the spirit and core of one's identity. When we hold back in one area of ourselves, we also hold back in other areas and a compromised life ensues. In holding back our truth, we are disloyal to the other person's spirit.

If you notice a fear of confrontation, then you must also notice what you seek to avoid is exactly what you are drawn to. This is a law of nature: nature always seeks a balance. Niceness soon destroys that which it initially set out to protect.

We have a craving to be known and to be accepted unconditionally, but first we must let ourselves be known by telling the people in our lives the truth of who we are. Our subconscious is appalled at this idea and it gives us all kinds of reasons to hold back. Mostly, we do hold back, never fulfilling our craving to be known. We feel sure that if we disclose our tender underbelly we will be attacked. Nevertheless, the only healthy option is to tell our truth, to trust ourselves to deal with the consequences and reactions of others. What I know for sure is that what you avoid is often what you will be drawn to.

Whom do you trust?

Almost everyone has had the experience of trusting the untrustworthy. Even the most sophisticated well-intentioned individuals are taken advantage of more times than they care to admit.

During a workshop he was leading, George Addair, founder and leader of the Omega Vector Training program, looked at me and said, "The extent that you trust others, is the extent to which you are trustworthy." I had an epiphany at that moment, and I have never been the same. From that moment on, I saw myself as ultimately responsible for me. I stopped blaming others for any aspect of my life. I understood his words this way: I can lead my life and make decisions according to my values because I can trust myself to deal with the consequences. I can deal with life on life's terms. If something great occurs, I will embrace it. If something disastrous occurs, I will walk through it with equanimity. I do not complain or whine, nor do I make others responsible for my emotional well-being. I just do what I do best and learn from the process.

This does not mean that I will not be exposed to untrustworthy people. The difference is that when I am ultimately trustworthy for myself, my intuition will nudge me in the correct direction, away from untrustworthy people. Moreover, if my intuition does fail as it sometimes does and I trust the untrustworthy, it will only be for small negative consequences, easily recoverable. In the past, when I trusted the untrustworthy, it took several incidences of my boundaries being crossed, sometimes at great financial or emotional cost, to look within myself for the root cause of this unfortunate trait. Now when I miss the mark and misplace my trust, I quickly change direction and recognize the lesson from the slip. As it happens, more often than not, when I have misplaced my trust it was because I was trying to take a fast forwarded route to love, success, friendship, or security. Because I was over-trusting, and making what I thought were gains to achieve something my hungry heart wanted, I did not correctly evaluate situations. I may even have had a gut instinct but because I wanted an easy win, I overrode those messages from my higher self. I see now that I had a *naive personality syndrome.* Although I have never seen any documentation on such syndrome, it is surely a good description of how I used to be!

Recently, I did an inventory of silly mistakes and poor decisions I made over the years of being in business and it came to over $65,000.00. That seems like a lot to me but when I tell other entrepreneurs about this they laugh and say it is just chicken scratch compared to their poor judgment. We all have experiences of trusting the untrustworthy. The point is to look through those situations, to see without judgment what role we played, forgive ourselves, and move on without self-recrimination. Although this is simple, it is not easy. But then, if it were easy everyone would be happy!

There is a New Age saying: If you see something in another that you don't like, take a look at yourself because it is part of you being reflected back through this other person. This is not necessarily true; however, the funny thing about a popular saying is that once it gains momentum it is believed to be true. The fact is that your negative perceptions about another person could just be your higher trustworthy self telling you, "Mayday, mayday, mayday! This person is not trustworthy."

When I was a little girl, there was a person in my community whose presence I just could not tolerate – I had an intense hatred for him. He never interfered with me in any way but I just could not stand to be around him. Much later, when I was a grown woman, we met and he bragged about randomly killing animals. Clearly, my higher self knew this penchant for this particular kind of evil all along and was giving me guidance. Since I am an animal activist, my revulsion for him then makes perfect sense to me now.

When we learn to make every experience a win, we are not afraid to make mistakes. We come to trust ourselves equally whether a decision has negative consequences or positive consequences. We believe this: I am trustworthy with myself. This resilience means we do not organize our lives to stay safe or to hear people exchange only pleasantries. Not that anything is wrong with pleasantries; it is just that a steady diet of them eventually becomes unappetizing.

Another positive effect of trusting ourselves is that we become less wary of people. Since we hold ourselves to be trustworthy, we presume that others with whom we come into contact are also trustworthy. This does not mean we become pushovers. It means we become more open to other opinions, even if those opinions are diametrically opposed to ours. Trusting does not mean we abandon our personal boundaries or our skill of discernment. Paradoxically, it also increases our ability to be discerning, to be able to decide more quickly if our intentions are a match.

According to Reinhard Bachman, professor of strategy at Surrey University's Business School in England and coauthor of the *Handbook of Trust Research*, "trust reduces complexities and ensures that we can swiftly maneuver the ambiguities of the day. In fact, because trust breeds efficiency, people who trust easily are more likely to experience more successes and power. Trusting saves time and effort that would otherwise go into attempting to control everything all the time."

I no longer *label* someone as trustworthy or untrustworthy. I simply notice dissimilar agendas and I trust myself fairly well, albeit not perfectly, to deal with untoward consequences. I agree with George's belief *to extent to which I am trustworthy with myself is the extent to which I am trustworthy with others.* Still, I give myself the right to take as much time as I need to bring a new person into my life. Too many of us have kept the front door of our houses locked but the door to our hearts wide open. Now, when I trust the wrong person I discover this fairly quickly and then I forgive myself by thinking, "Oops, my person picker must have been <u>temporarily</u> out of service."

This reminds me of a Seinfeld episode where Elaine, who when she discovered her favorite contraceptive sponges were about to be discontinued, went to hundreds of pharmacies in New York, bought up their stock and stockpiled them for future use. From there on, whenever she met a man to whom she was attracted, and knowing she had a diminishing supply of contraception, would ask herself this question before taking that next step, "He's really cute but is he sponge-worthy?"

It would not set us back if we stepped aside from the allure of someone new, either business or personal, and asked ourselves two questions. The first, *is he/she trustworthy* and just as importantly, *what is it about me that wants to be rescued by him or her?*

Trusting the Untrustworthy

Trusting the untrustworthy is a common weakness. Even the most sophisticated, well-informed individuals are taken advantage of more times than they care to admit. This is unjust and unfair, but so what? The trend will not change unless we learn to ask ourselves this all-important question: What is it about me that causes me to trust the untrustworthy?

Telltale signs to discern if you trust the untrustworthy:

- I make decisions quickly.
- I am unable to take the time for due diligence.
- I make decisions based on how great my need is to be rescued from something.
- I crave change and am impatient with process.
- I am unable to deal with my own uncomfortable feelings when I see someone in need.
- I need to be liked.
- I have a hungry heart; I seek approval and rescue rather than self-care.

When you discover your reasons for trusting the untrustworthy, plan to spend some time in quiet reflection. See if you can determine how and where you contributed to almost every situation that hurt you. This does not mean it is open season – beating yourself up is not the answer. It is more a matter of believing, "Oh, so that's the cause. Now I need to learn new skills so it does not happen again."

To reduce the danger of trusting the untrustworthy, one of the tools you can put to work right now is a balance sheet listing the pros and cons of any decision you are about to make. Give yourself a week just to sit with the process and ask some "call to truth" questions:

- When have you been let down?
- Are you facing a similar situation now?
- What is the cost of doing (or having) this?
- What is the cost of not doing (not having) this?
- If I wait a few days will my need and desire be as great, or will I want it less?
- Who could potentially lose because of this decision?
- Do I want to be rescued from a difficult situation?

Most decisions made in a hurry turn out to be wrong. Interestingly, fraudulent people are usually in a hurry to build our trust. Your new mantra could be, "I make my decisions over time, with lots of due diligence." Another step is to require the other person to put in writing, in measurable terms, what they will be delivering. If they cannot or will not, the answer is clear – Mayday! Mayday! Mayday!

Context and Vulnerability

Most people do not deliberately set out to mislead each other. What is more likely is that they intend to communicate unequivocally but that intention is clouded by a hidden agenda to be safe (the unconscious at work again).

If people are not able to stand back and receive feedback without becoming emotionally hooked, where they defend and justify their actions or attitudes, they will not be able to admit their own truth to themselves. This works in reverse as well: If I squelch my truth, I will squelch yours.

Personally, I prefer to be told the truth directly and clearly. It would be wonderful if all truth could be expressed without emotional spill over, but since there is no guarantee of this, I will gladly accept emotional spill over rather than no truth at all.

Two techniques can help us be gracious and tell the truth in a dignified and respectful manner. One technique involves creating a context and the other technique involves what I call deliberate vulnerability.

Technique #1: Create a Context

It is possible to tell almost anyone almost anything if we first support the relationship at the start of the conversation. You might say something like this, "Janice, you really add value to the team by challenging the status quo and focusing us on the agenda. There is something I need to discuss, if that is alright with you. When you interrupted me, I felt discounted. My sense is that you were impatient and disinterested in my opinion. How do you see the situation? I promise not to get angry or defensive."

There are five parts to a respectful confrontation:

1. Support the relationship…"Susan, we have worked together for five years and I appreciate how efficient you are when it comes to logistics. I can always be secure in the knowledge that you will not let the important deadlines be missed."
2. And there is a situation I would like to chat with you about… when you _____,
3. I feel _____,
4. And my sense is that you_____
5. Tell me how you feel about that and I promise to respond to whatever you say by being silent or by saying thank you.

Step five is vital because too many of us have asked for someone's opinion and when they give it to us we have been defensive. Because of that, we have the attitude: once burned; twice shy.

Technique #2: Deliberate Vulnerability

Deliberate vulnerability means we put the possibility that we are wrong into our assessment of the issues. Consider these statements:

1. I may not be right about this but ...
2. Let me tell you what I think, if it's okay with you, and you tell me how you see it.
3. Does this sound fair to you?
4. If it's okay with you, I'd like to give you some feedback.
5. I may be way out in left field here but ...

Using phrases like these limit the force of the other person's defense mechanisms and encourage him or her to accept what you are saying. You build trust and enhance the relationship by showing respect before entering into an emotionally charged discussion. Although this process is simple, it is not easy.

Chapter XI

TRUTH CONNECTS

*T*ELLING THE TRUTH ALLOWS PEOPLE IN A RELATIONSHIP TO BUILD TRUST. TRUTH BONDS PEOPLE TOGETHER AND CREATES ENDURING RELATIONSHIPS.

The Truth Is Best to Be Told

Developing a process for telling our truth in a graceful and elegant manner gives us fewer reasons to feel resentment because issues and concerns can be dealt with as they arise. In addition, those with whom we communicate are not so readily stung by our words because our words are delivered with the intention of connecting and improving the relationship. A person who feels generosity, love, and peace of mind expresses the very same emotions to others.

When we live for something bigger than we are, we do not worry about payoffs at the mechanical level. The only way to get to a higher place is by achieving more peace of mind. However, taking pain and frustration away does not give us peace of mind because we are then no longer motivated. Without pain and frustration, we are content to rest on our laurels. Working through the angst, pain, and frustration of fear actually buys us freedom and personal mastery.

When we live by defensiveness, resentment, and judgment we experience survival. Survival is not enough. Survival is what the pioneers and early explorers did when they came to North America more than 150 years ago. Survival is our own personal, private, ever-present, familiar hell on earth. When we choose to act graciously to others, even in the presence of a glaring defect, we go beyond survival into finesse.

Sadly, we expect time to change our experience. We tell ourselves, "If I wait out this bad phase, then I will have a good relationship. When the kids are gone, then we will get close." Our experience of life, however, is not improved on a timeline. Those fine changes only come about if we are shocked out of our comfort (agony) zone. In other words, we move from the comfort zone to the growing zone. Then we learn new and effective skills, skills that serve others in our lives not just us. It is vital that we identify when our behaviors have become defense mechanisms that do not serve us anymore. We might ask ourselves, "Does this behavior serve just me, or does it serve others as well?" More often than not, our defenses serve only ourselves.

Being reflective is difficult for most people because it asks us to reveal a level of truth about ourselves that may be unfamiliar, or uncomfortable. Telling other people superficial information about ourselves is easy, compared to telling ourselves a higher level of truth about the person we see in the mirror. This higher level of truth includes unmasking our fears, doubts, insecurities, and weaknesses. A weakness is a strength waiting to be transformed.

Rigorous honesty is vital if we want to move to the top rung on the ladder of self-mastery. Self-honesty is the most difficult form of honesty. Denial by its very function is self-defense in retrospect. An enlightened person might say, "I was in denial about understanding my class assignment. I wonder what else I am in denial about?" You can see this person is becoming open to change. When we are entrenched in denial, we are unaware of possibilities because we have well-honed defenses to counter our weaknesses. I saw a t-shirt recently that read, *Denial is not just a river in Egypt.*

Being un-teachable is as if we are wearing a banner declaring, "Keep away. Only gentle truths permitted here." Those gentle truths support our defense of denial. Once our minds are open to a range of possibilities about a situation, we are more humble and teachable. When we are in this state of openness, our willingness may quicken our development. We may learn more in six months than in years of study with conferences, seminars and books. Being willing and teachable allows our teachers, who have always been there, to approach us.

Lying for Self-Protection

Lying to others is our first line of defense. It brought us safety when we were little and it still buys us protection as adults.

Mary is an 18 month-old sitting in her highchair. She spilled some milk from her cup and looked in wonder at her new creation – a white puddle. Without too much fuss her mother wiped it up and gave her some more. Mary could not resist the creative urge and deliberately spilled her milk again. Mom, not amused, admonished her young daughter. The next week, by accident this time, milk spilled again. "Who did that?" Mom asked with reproach in her voice. Mary shook her head, "Not me." Mary was doing what she could to avoid being confronted by her mother's displeasure.

As children, we learned to lie largely because we were powerless to deal with the criticism – the shaming and blaming – of adults. Although we are not children anymore, we still instinctively make excuses or lie to protect ourselves, even when the truth would be more appropriate. Truth, in fact, is enabling.

It is vital to tell our own truth. This process of telling ourselves the truth is interesting. It is certainly a delicate process. Here's an example:

I received a sixth call from the manager of a rapidly growing insurance brokerage firm regarding sales training and overcoming the fear of cold calling. Over the previous year I prepared two proposals, spent three long meetings with the employees, negotiated on price, and the manager still asked for yet another proposal. Usually my investment of time for this scope of work included a maximum of two meetings and one follow-up letter confirming cost, dates, and other logistics.

If I had told myself the truth in the beginning, I would have thought, *something about this manager gives me an uncomfortable feeling.* However, I did not want to hear that because I had an agenda to get the deal. Finally, however, I developed the courage to tell the client (and myself) the truth: I am unwilling to provide another proposal. I had no regrets about finally telling the truth (a truth that I could have told in the beginning) by simply saying, "You know, I do not think we are a match."

This choice could have evolved from a sense of discernment, instead of judgment, if only I had been willing to trust my instinct, but my zeal for the deal took over. What held me back was fear of economic insecurity. The lesson I learned was: *fear of economic insecurity causes economic insecurity.* A case in point is a friend who fed her male cat no-name brand food. I suggested that she switch to a higher quality brand due to male cats having a problem with urinary tract infections. She declined, and was faced with a $750 vet bill one year later.

Strategic Honesty

Strategic honesty is important and achievable when you step back from the stimulus. But why be strategic? Is being strategically honest compatible with being rigorously honest? Yes! Strategic honesty means combining timing and tact with truth. You have a delicate objective: to develop a strong relationship through elegant truth-telling. A relationship without truth is only a truce. If a relationship cannot withstand your truth, then it is probably not a healthy relationship.

Truth blurted out or given spontaneously in anger will likely close down the other person. Dealing with someone's anger, the aftermath of blurting out blunt truth, may require more time spent restoring the relationship than you care to invest. The other option is to take a few minutes and consider a strategic approach to communicating your message.

To be strategically honest, you must choose words and a tone that will be respectful. If you are able to step back, take stock, and create the space, emotionally and temporally, in which to develop an understanding and connection, rather than a misunderstanding and disconnection, you will mitigate unpleasant defensiveness and posturing. You can develop an inner sense of self-regard by speaking consciously, by giving your word and keeping it.

When you give your word and do not keep it, you are acting outside of integrity. You are being incongruent and untrustworthy. Can you keep your word one hundred percent of the time? Of course not; yet even when you cannot keep your word, you can still be accountable.

There is only one test to tell if someone is congruent, and that is the test of time. When we give our word to ourselves and to others and keep it, we are perceived to be trustworthy. We are known by our actions. When our words and actions match, we are congruent and trustworthy. Being one hundred percent accountable and responsible puts us in a position of inner power. No one else can destroy our grace and equanimity. When we lose grace, we are uncoordinated with life. Our discomfort becomes so acute, so painful, we are immediately motivated to take corrective action.

By taking responsibility for ourselves, our positive and our negative behavior, we create a form of living immunity.

If we remain healthy in an environment where people are succumbing to smallpox or any other disease, we are considered to have immunity. The same is true when we are able to avoid falling apart inside (or outside) when others mock, reject or project anything unpleasant onto us. We have a form of living immunity, or self-containment which allows us to walk among the masses with their insecurities, their inclinations to be resentful and angry, to blame and to shame, and not be depleted of energy.

The function of an automobile's alternator is to keep the battery charged while the engine is running. If the alternator is broken, the battery becomes depleted of its energy. The driver is unaware of this until the automobile shudders to a halt. Like an alternator, self-containment and self-regard will give you the ability to maintain your own energy, moving quickly to tap the leak when you sense yourself stalled by the defenses of others. A forgiving attitude contributes to living immunity. Challenges and upsets will still occur. It is just that we will not become co-opted by the drama of the stressful scenario.

When we are clear with ourselves and others, and we give permission to others to be clear and candid with us, we contribute to our own self-regard. Imagine having the ability to receive all forms of feedback, both critical and complimentary, and to communicate clearly when misunderstandings occur, to quickly clear things up without sadness or drama.

Doing our best and taking responsibility when we mess up keeps our inner alternator working properly. It keeps our energy from leaking out all over the place. The point is to question ourselves, "Was this my best, or did I settle for good enough?" If the answer is the latter, go back and add to the last effort. See how self-regard grows from taking responsibility. Self-regard cannot be bought, learned at a workshop or acquired by reading a book. It comes from taking chances, doing our best, making mistakes, learning from them and then trying again.

How can people cope well with life on life's terms when their self-regard has not evolved to the level of self-trust? They do so by moving toward their insecurity and embracing it. The following story illustrates why I love my insecurities.

When I first began my career as a professional speaker and corporate trainer, I was hired along with two other trainers to conduct a series of workshops. I approached one of the other trainers in a friendly manner. She was not impressed and was, in fact, distant. Intimidated, I said to myself, "She must be good. I am in exalted company here." In preparing for my workshop I worked extra hard, digging deep down and going the extra mile.

A month or so later I ran into her at the movies. Again, I was like a friendly puppy. Again, she was reserved. "That's it!" I told myself, feeling fear, doubt, and more than a normal amount of insecurity, "She's in the process of landing a contract with the client. I must be even more diligent in my follow-up and my next proposal."

Because of my insecurity, I worked extra hard. I was more diligent in my preparations than if I had been basking in confidence. And in the end my contract was continued by that company for several years. In addition, as the participants in my workshops moved on, I was invited to work with their organizations. To this day I am still in contact with some of those people whose disapproval I initially feared. How often do we compare ourselves to others and find ourselves wanting, even retreating from the game? We compare our insides with someone else's outsides. So what? Go ahead and do that if it helps, but then leverage your insecurity.

Self-confidence is good but it does not go far enough. Confidence is the feeling we have just before we understand the situation, and leveraging those insecurities will get us further than basking in the glow of self-confidence. We become courageous if we transform our insecurities into assets. However, here is the main confidence trigger: that emotion is our friend, fear!

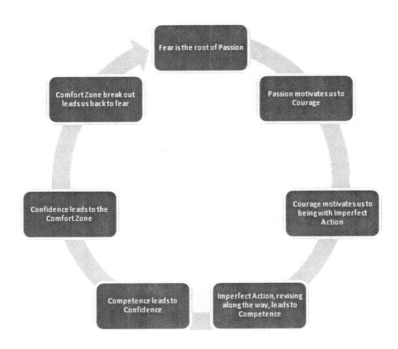

If we fear telling someone our truth but do so anyway, we are courageous. This contributes to our personal greatness. Everything we want is on the other side of fear.

Along with personal greatness comes resiliency which is that certain something, that inner strength, we can draw on to help us deal with the difficulties we encounter in life. Those distressing events, paradoxically contribute to our personal greatness in the first place. You may have observed someone who can handle life on life's terms. Rest assured that person is not without strife and struggles – not at all! He or she has challenges and setbacks and yet deals with them with equanimity, calmness, and grace.

It takes no courage, when faced with someone lashing out at us, to lash back. That is the reaction of a coward. Courage comes from holding our tongues, from managing our behavior to the highest standards. To our lower selves, our selves that are overrun by fear, attacking the attacker seems justified. Using conscious choice and responding to the attack with grace and discernment is the stronger and more spiritual choice.

When we repeatedly and consciously choose our reaction, we create inner strength and resiliency. This does not mean we support, condone or hang around others who attack and criticize. Rather, it means we manage ourselves while we are exposed. We become safe with ourselves – resilient, mended, strong at the broken places, bendable like willows instead of snapping like dry twigs. When we are resilient, it is easier to keep our hearts attuned to our dreams and goals.

Telling the truth

Sometimes people say, "I didn't tell you the truth because I didn't want to hurt your feelings." This is a disrespectful statement. It is disrespectful because the people who say this are pre-judging how others will react. They make assumptions about the reaction of others to the truth and they believe their assumptions to be true. In not telling the truth, they are denying the other person's reality and his or her honest response to that reality.

When people say to you, "I would have told you the truth but I didn't want to hurt your feelings," they assume you are not strong enough to deal with the truth. They predict a negative reaction from you and they project their erroneous beliefs onto you. If you decline to tell me the truth to protect my feelings, I would feel patronized and insulted. Here are three reasons why:

- Who are you to decide for me what will and will not hurt my feelings?
- Who are you to decide that handling those feelings is not the growth I need right now?

- You did not trust me to deal with your truth in a spiritually elegant manner. In essence, you pre-judged me as a retaliatory person, one who would get even with someone for saying something upsetting.

The truth is we lie because we don't know how to tell the truth in a respectful manner. If someone retaliates with defensiveness, whose feelings get hurt? The one doing the telling! So it is our own feelings we protect. Go ahead, take a chance and express your true self. If you're not perfect, you can ask for forgiveness.

The more you tell the truth about what you believe, think, and feel, the more honest others will be with you. Then you will be dealing with the reality of life on life's terms, instead of life being a moving target where you are never sure of your values, or where you truthfully stand on important issues. When we are truthful there is less to forgive.

Marketing research shows that to build trust with others we need to have several meaningful contacts with them. How many times do we say, "I love you" to the people we love? We say it repeatedly because it builds trust, receptivity, bonding, and it provides reassurance. Telling the truth is vitally important because when we do not tell the truth we know others do not respect us for our true selves. We know deep down that we are projecting an illusion and if we are being accepted based on an illusion, the relationship is on shaky ground.

Seven Steps for Telling the Truth

Wouldn't it be wonderful if there was a process by which we could tell our truth in a safe and respectful manner? Wouldn't it be wonderful if there was a process that made us feel honored, that our friends and partners trusted us enough to share what is really happening with them? The good news is there is such a process and I'm going to share it with you here.

These seven easy steps for telling the truth are important because they provide a rational solution to a delicate emotional issue. By using this process you will be able to tell almost anything to almost anyone with grace and elegance. This seven step prescription shows how to share your truth in a way that allows you to maintain self-respect while respecting the emotions of others. When you do not tell the truth, you are not respected for your authentic self. You know deep down that you are projecting an illusion.

Step #1: Know When to Tell the Truth

A good rule of thumb is to hold your tongue until you have asked yourself these questions:

- Do I want to tell the truth so that I can get closer to this person?
- Am I telling the truth because I want to know this person better, to move forward and have a stronger relationship?
- Am I coming from the highest intention or do I just want to get something off my chest?
- If I tell the truth, will this person still have the right to be authentic in his or her response to me?

It is important to ask these questions because the answers will reveal the integrity of your intentions. If your intentions are rife with hidden agendas – to make someone feel small so you can feel big, or to make someone feel dumb so you can feel smart – there is no reason to have the conversation. Either you must walk away or you must elevate your intentions. This step can make all of the difference in your communication skills. It is also a good idea to ask you the following questions:

- What is the problem?
- Whose problem is it?

- Is this my business?
- If not, why am I using my energy to invest in a drama that does not affect me?

These questions bring us to the delicate place of combining caring with acceptance, and respect with detachment. Detaching from dramas that are not ours is usually the respectful thing to do. When we jump in to solve someone's problem we may be rescuing that person from a lesson he or she needs to learn.

Usually, the one who created the mess is the one most competent to deal with it. We can show support by letting the person know that we will be there if help is needed, but that we are not in the driver's seat. In addition, just because someone asks for help or advice does not mean he or she must act on that. Ideally, we will be able to help the person find his or her best solution.

As an aside, another relationship that could use this approach is the relationship we have with ourselves. Far too often we say or think things about ourselves that would be appalling if spoken about us by anyone else.

Step #2: Validate and Support the Relationship

Before you begin to discuss a delicate situation, you need to do the best you can to ensure the other person does not go into a defensive state. You can prevent this perfectly human reaction by saying something such as, "I value the years of experience you bring to the team and I want us to continue working together." By first supporting the relationship, it is possible to tell almost anyone almost anything, critical or not, and to have it accepted.

Recently I attended a workshop where as a learning experience we were asked to wander around the classroom, shaking hands with others and saying, "I love and respect you but I do not care if you like me." (The actual wording was much harsher than this!) I understood the point. We were being encouraged to give up the need to be people pleasers. Yet, there is a way to stand in our own truth with grace without attacking the other person. Supporting the relationship by validating the other person lowers both sets of defenses. It softens the edges, creating a safety net for the vulnerable feelings that are sure to be exposed by both parties.

Step #3: Give Choice

Ask permission to bring up the delicate subject. Say something like this, "I'd like to discuss a delicate subject, if that's alright with you. You may feel uncomfortable – I know I will – but it is a small issue that needs a bit of discussion. Is now a good time or would later be better?" Usually the person will say, "Right now." He or she may feel anxiety and that's okay. Just don't make it worse by being adamant and fierce. Be as relaxed as you can.

Step #4: Create a Disclaimer

It is important to remember that whatever truth you tell comes from your own perceptions. It is not necessarily true for anyone else. Preface your statement by acknowledging what you are about to say is your own perception of the issue. As I discussed in the previous chapter, you might say:

- My sense is ...
- It seems to me ...
- I may be out in left field ...
- This is my perception ...

Never, ever speak for others. Sometimes people say, "It's not only me. Everyone else feels the same way I do." This is just a way of building our defenses by co-opting others into our drama. Maybe others feel the same as you. That is their business to be telling, not yours. Can someone else represent you as you can? Occasionally someone will become the messenger, voicing concerns for a whole team. That person acts as the mouthpiece for the group but after the confrontation the messenger turns to his peers for support only to be presented with silence all around. You've probably heard the expression, "Don't shoot the messenger." In this case, the messenger shot himself. Don't be cowardly. Tell your own truth without the backup of others. Truth stands on its own. It needs no defense.

Step #5: Speak in First Person

Truth needs to be expressed in the first person. It takes no courage to tell someone else's truth. It is easy to confront someone with a statement like this, "You are really arrogant! You think you are better than anyone else!"

Putting that statement in "I" language might appear as, "When we are in the monthly department meeting and you interrupt, I feel discounted. Then I shut down, and I regret that. Is there some feedback you would like to give me about my style of presentation or its content? Please be candid. I promise not to become defensive. I really would value your input, and my only response will be to thank you."

First-person truth-telling language begins with I, me, my:

- This is what I saw ...
- These are my perceptions ...
- My judgments are ...
- I sense ...

If someone gives us feedback that hurts our feelings or offends us, we can choose to use it to solidify our value of honest communication. In addition, we may feel bad, sad, hurt, mad, etc. So what? Self-government means we feel these emotions and maintain our equilibrium anyway. As an added bonus, we get better at it and now the opportunity exists, due to honesty, to create the very beginnings of a relationship with this other person based on a firm foundation where none existed before.

There is a freedom in telling the truth which allows people to live with more reality and less illusion.

Telling the truth is simple, but not easy. If it were, we would have no need for defenses or pretenses. As children, we often heard our parents admonishing us to *tell the truth!* However, they rarely modeled how to tell the truth by speaking in the first person. Instead, the proclamations of our parents included phrases like, "You are lazy!" or "You are doing that wrong," or "You've messed up again!" When we heard these statements, however well intentioned, our little spirits were diminished and our feelings were hurt. We came to realize that being told what we thought was the truth would result in hurt feelings. Often we also came to believe what we were told. Why wouldn't we have believed what our parents told us?

I saw a bumper sticker that said, "A Happy Childhood Lasts Forever." Sadly, the reverse is also true. As adults, our need to be liked often conflicts with our desire to tell the truth, and all too often our need to be liked wins. Because we were never shown a respectful process for truth telling, we stumble along doing the best we can or we remain silent. Too many of us compromise ourselves by not telling the naked truth for the sake of our relationships. As I alluded to in the previous section, a valuable belief is, "I appreciate myself enough *not to* care about what other people think about me, and to have the willingness to be misunderstood."

After developing a context for myself around truth-telling, I now let people know one of my core values is that I am not willing to maintain the relationship if it means not being true to myself. Funnily enough, many of my friends now call and say, "I need an opinion and I know I can trust you to tell me the truth."

Step #6: Offer an Opportunity to Receive Feedback

When you ask for feedback, cushion your request with the promise that you will not become defensive. Reassure the other person by saying something like this, "This is how I see the situation. I would be very interested in your point of view and I promise, no matter what you say, I will not be defensive."

This step is critical if you expect anyone to give rigorously honest feedback because it lets the other person know you will accept any response without retaliation. When others know they are safe to give me feedback of any kind without retaliation, they are more likely to be truthful. This is vital for anyone who expects others to be truthful to them.

Almost everyone has given feedback only to have it thrown back in their face with defenses and arguments. It probably will not happen if you treat the other person with respect as outlined in these steps, but it is best to be prepared for the possibility a small percentage will become defensive and retaliate. When someone does react defensively, know that time will heal the hurt and remind yourself you came from the highest intention.

Step #7: Reflect and Plan

Review the information presented by you and the other person. List what you learned and develop a plan to move forward. Come to a mutual agreement about steps to resolve the issue. Agree on a date to follow up with each other to review progress.

Learning how to tell the truth with equanimity and grace takes time. But imagine being the opposite – someone who makes up stories in order to manage others' opinions of them. One instance when people do not tell the absolute truth is when they are late. Notice how some people will blame their lateness on external causes. Excuses include bad traffic, someone called just as they were leaving, or the alarm didn't go off. An excuse is not the truth. Even though a fantastical story does not make up for being late, not many people will hold the tardy person accountable.

The opposite scenario describes someone who has learned that the best way to deal with being late is to ascribe inside, versus outside, accountability. An example of this is to own your lateness by saying something like, "I was late because I am disorganized today and completely misjudged how long it would take to get here. Please forgive me for not keeping our time commitment."

If you choose the first scenario you will appear as flaky, unreliable, and ultimately untrustworthy. In addition, when you make excuses instead of telling the truth you appear to have a lack of integrity in relation to giving your word and keeping it.

Telling the truth, even if it feels like you are making yourself look bad in the moment, will increase your self-esteem and improve relationships with your friends and associates. You will be seen as a center of influence and be able to tap into the good graces of others.

Chapter XII

TRUST WITH TIME

*T*HE EXPERIENCES WE SHARE WITH OTHERS PROVIDE OPPORTUNITIES TO GET TO KNOW EACH OTHER. THIS SHARING ALLOWS FOR GROWTH BASED ON TIME INVESTED.

Truth Builds Trust in a Relationship

It takes time to bond with another person. We need to establish trust in business, friendships, intimate relationships, and in teams. When a relationship is secure, each partner assumes some responsibility for maintaining its structure. In the interim, while the relationship is building, it is our responsibility to show up in our full integrity. I am not suggesting that you tell too much too soon or become too committed too soon. I am suggesting that you act trustworthy no matter how the other person acts. Be an observer and notice if he or she lives by his or her word. Listen to words but count on actions because actions speak louder than words. Give yourself the gift of time to determine to what extent someone is trustworthy and, therefore, worthy of your continued investment. This can be part of your self-care plan!

No Truth	→	No Trust
No Trust	→	No Respect
No Respect	→	No Relationship

Well, it is not that no relationship will exist. It's just that the relationship will be dysfunctional because none of the participants can be free to express his or her authentic thoughts, feelings or beliefs.

The A.R.T. of Living:
Accountability with Responsibility equals Trustworthy

"Be one hundred percent responsible for one hundred percent of my life," you say? I can imagine you wrestling with that concept, so let us discuss it. Assuming one hundred percent responsibility might seem like a formula to ensure that you face life alone, without the support of others. Think about the words of a popular Simon and Garfunkel song, "I am a rock, I am an island." Who wants that?

Yes, there are many situations in life over which you have no control. In those situations where you feel powerless you have three choices. The choices are to adopt either a submissive, defensive, or fully accepting stance. The third choice, acting as if you accept ultimate responsibility actually increases your options. You might be surprised at the amount of power you have to change yourself, to change your circumstances, and to influence others simply by assuming the attitude and behavior of accepting responsibility for your feelings, thoughts and actions. As well, you need to take responsibility for what you say about what happens to you, thereby avoiding victimhood!

Let's say you promised to complete a job on July 17, and it is now July 12 but you have come to a dead end. You don't know how to accomplish an important part of that job, yet you are one hundred percent responsible. What should you do?

The answer is to ask for help. In doing so, you still maintain one hundred percent responsibility. Asking for help is actually accepting responsibility.

Now imagine a team brought together to accomplish a task. The team leader presents the objectives along with the desired outcomes. Everyone on the team personally and voluntarily accepts (for no one can mandate this to another) one hundred percent responsibility for the result. This is imperative for a great team to function.

100% Accountable + 100% Responsible = 100% Trustworthy
75% Accountable + 75% Responsible = 75% Trustworthy
50% Accountable + 50% Responsible = 50% Trustworthy

A relationship in which each of the partners assumes one hundred percent of the responsibility functions better than a relationship in which one partner accepts only partial responsibility. Imagine saying to a chain, "Okay, you three links are only fifty percent responsible, but all you other links are one hundred percent responsible." With lowered responsibility, the efficacy of the entire chain is lowered. Would you want a chain with three weak links holding back a pair of ferocious guard dogs in your neighbor's yard? Probably not!

It takes courage to accept one hundred percent responsibility for our lives. If I assign eighty-five percent responsibility to me and fifteen percent responsibility to you, I am in a potential victim state for your fifteen percent.

Assuming responsibility for our participation in the past frees us from projecting guilt and resentment onto others. Let's say someone did something bad to you as a child. How can you take one hundred percent responsibility? You can do this by saying, "This bad thing happened and I can let it affect me for the rest of my life, or I can choose one hundred percent responsibility for my attitude toward it. I can observe how my thinking about the past event colors my life today. I do not like or want that, so I let go. The past is done – I cannot change it. It does not exist. If I continue to live there, I am controlled by an illusion, for an illusion is something that does not exist but that I give energy to anyway."

Taking one hundred percent responsibility for the present is a relief. When something bad occurs, there seems to be a frenzied witch-hunt – who shall we blame for this? What if someone stepped up to the plate and said, "Let's stop looking for the person who did this, and start looking for the solution."

Like the past, the future is also an illusion. It is not here yet but we can be prepared and give ourselves the edge by assuming one hundred percent responsibility for ourselves as we go forward. With this proactive attitude we have focus. This is one of the reasons top performers achieve their position. They have a concrete plan for their lives. They have already taken the time to create priorities for the future. There is something magical about that. Our expectations have a greater chance of being achieved when we plan.

In addition, with a plan we give ourselves the freedom to add, delete, or change in response to actual events (as compared to planned events). If we have no plan and leave everything up to fate, we must blindly accept what comes and fit ourselves to it as best we can. When we have a plan life still delivers tragedy and sorrow, but when it does we are resilient and not thrown off course for long. Our attitude of living one hundred percent responsibly keeps us vigilant.

The quicker we assume responsibility for the solution, the more likely we will see ourselves and be seen by others as having the traits of a leader. The future will provide us with freedom, abundance, challenge, reward, pain, setbacks, joy, and success, all of which make up the rich tapestry of life. Do not spend time affixing blame. Fix the problem!

I recently had the experience of renovating an investment property. When the general contractor's pre-allotted time was up, I turned to our local 'cash corner' for help. This particular corner is where homeless and/ or unemployed men stand around looking for daily work for cash. Luck was on my side because the first day I chose two men, Bob and Frank, to help me. Their job was to dig a large trench so I could install a window in the basement. The trench was 5 feet long, 3 feet wide, and 4 feet deep, and the first 18 inches were through frozen ground.

Bob, although he worked hard, told me a long, detailed story blaming and criticizing others for his situation. He was not invited back. Frank, who also worked hard, blamed no one. Needless to say, it was Frank who continued to work for me until the project was completed, and he did a fantastic job.

As it happens, Frank is a graphic artist who used to own a print and sign shop in Montreal. I was drawn to work with Frank long before I knew about his skills, other than digging ditches. Frank's attitude, self-government, and unwillingness to blame anyone else resulted in being able to avoid the cash corner throughout the coldest months of winter. Now Frank places a higher value on his time and services and has plans to proceed with his own painting business. My referrals alone will provide a great start at his new business. Responsibility and accountability were the key components needed to investing complete trust in him.

Chapter XIII

VICTIM OR AGENT

We have heard much about being a victim but little about the opposite state, agency, and the ability to be empowered.

Living Life to its Fullest

People who are not in charge, who cannot influence others to affect their lives positively, are victims. People who are in a state of agency can not only take care of themselves, they can take care of others and positively affect their living standards.

An emotionally charged situation is a stimulus for a response. What will this response be? Will you react defensively or will you question, seeking to understand and to maintain emotional control? Will you stay in your own circle of benevolent power or will you leak your power by justifying and defending? Will you be a victim of your own fears or will you be your own best agent? Victims believe that the state of mind or state of life they are experiencing is the direct responsibility of some external force. Victims suffer from destructive or injurious actions. They are deceived or cheated by the dishonesty of others. In contrast, agents are people or organizations that thrive by taking care of others. An agent can also be a company that has a franchise to represent another. Agency is the state of being in action, and of exerting power and influence.

Agency Model

How life looks when we have an agency attitude:

- Lives life on life's terms instead of complaining, blaming, or worrying.
- If something goes wrong and causes upset, an agent takes 100% responsibility for feelings, emotions, and actions.
- Goes into action and finds solution.
- Experiences results of solution and makes any necessary adjustments.

Let us assume someone in your department annoys you with peculiar habits and mannerisms. You could move out of victim mode by asking, "What is it about me that makes me annoyed by her? What is it about me that cannot ignore her?"

The answer might be a need (or habit) to feel judgmental and superior. Then the question becomes, "What is it about me that makes me need to feel superior?" The answer might be, "I get to feel more powerful because within my job, relationships or some other areas in my life I feel powerless." Then, when you have come to this realization, you can look at those areas in which you feel powerless and be responsible for enacting positive changes.

Given that an outside agency's role is to be a positive influence, what would it be like to be "in agency" for ourselves? The only requirement for us to become an agent is to take one hundred percent responsibility for ourselves. No one has taught us how to do this. Instead, we learn to justify, defend, blame, shame, and make excuses. Taking one hundred percent responsibility is empowering. More than any other concrete, personal change we could make, it brings us closer to our core.

Michael Korda has written several books and articles about personal and professional power. After reading his ideas, I realized that powerful people seem to be comforted by displays of power in other people. Yet when we feel intimidated or insecure around powerful people we clam up. We make ourselves small, so as not to annoy or upset them. We think they have intimidated us but, really, we shrink inside our turmoil of emotions and become victims, instead of going into agency mode and claiming our space and our right to be there.

Remember the movie *Jerry McGuire*? Jerry McGuire was an agent. He earned his income and took care of himself and his family by taking care of a professional football player. If we were in a position to afford it, having someone on the payroll whose sole function is to take care of us would be great. Most of us do not enjoy this luxury, however, so we need to become an agent for ourselves, to be in a constant state of "self agency".

My program, *Cold Calling Strategies for Chickens, Cowards and the Faint-of-Heart,* is intended for those in the selling profession who want to prospect and make cold calls but do not do so because they fear rejection. When they do tap into their courage to make prospecting calls they are in agency mode, in a position of exerting power and influence. When salespeople or entrepreneurs are behind in their business goals, those who are willing to prospect by cold calling can move into action, or agency, and do what they need to do, even though to get the job done they must face the fear of rejection. Deciding *not to* make the cold call, even if success depends on it, is to be a victim of one's own feelings and emotions.

Note that the definition of agency does not say, "To be in perfect action", but rather, any action, even action that causes us to succeed, to fail, or any aspect in between contributes to the process of developing personal power, because the failure shows us what does not work. We can then make the appropriate changes and move on. Unfortunately, victims (people who believe that they do not have personal power or do not know how to activate it) repeatedly do the same thing repeatedly and expect different results.

In sales, victims hope that referrals will come but they end up languishing in mediocrity. In other areas of business, victims may hope for a promotion but do little to see that it comes to fruition. Those who think that perfectionism is a lofty goal are victims of their own belief systems. Procrastinators want it done just right but they never quite get the time. These folks sit in judgment of those of us who do try and who make mistakes. Perfectionists sit back safely in their cradles of competence, not daring to take a chance and experience the imperfection of learning new tasks.

In the example of the salesperson that needed to make cold calls, it is better to attempt the call in all its imperfections than to wait until the perfect script is prepared, the perfect prospect is identified, and the sun, stars, and moon are all aligned! Being consistent with imperfect action will often yield astoundingly successful rewards. Whoever told you perfection was the goal was probably told the same thing by parents or others in authority. Without questioning the meaning, without thinking about the impact of such a pronouncement, the authority figure passed it on to you. Perfectionism and procrastination are simply the opposite sides of the same coin so *if you show me a perfectionists I will show you a procrastinator!*

When you are committed to doing your best learning, your mistakes must become "So what?" moments, just as successful events become "So what?" moments. Whatever the results, it is important to keep challenging your comfort zone.

The salesperson that makes a mistake during a cold call must immediately move on to the next call, staying in agency mode. To give up and go into self-recrimination in response to the unsatisfactory call means adopting victim behavior. To claim our fair share, the time has come to move beyond victim to agent. There is enough in the world for everyone, and that includes you and me.

Moving from victim takes awareness and time. We must first admit that we sometimes abdicate responsibility for our lives and our feelings to others. When they do not do the job we want them to do, we blame them and hold resentment. That attitude places us securely in the victim mode.

More often, we do not get what we want in life because of specific choices we make. Most of the situations we get into are actually negotiated events (by default). Not taking responsibility, manifested by not asking for what we want, means we default to accepting what we get, even if it is unacceptable. When our results are less than desirable, we need to ask some hard questions:

- What choices did I make to cause the chain of events that led to this?
- What is it about me that created this?
- What is it about me that resists taking a chance?
- What is it about me that doesn't ask respectfully and directly for what I want?

Remember, big questions yield big answers, and any question that begins with: "What is it about me that ...," is a big question!

The One Percent Solution

Whatever you decide to do with your time, ten years from now you will be ten years older. Why not use that time to move forward, instead of staying stuck in feelings from the past – that quagmire of remorse, disappointment, and doubt? It is better to leverage painful feelings by deciding to embrace them and move through them.

If I offer you a penny today and promise to double that penny each day, will you work for me? If you decline, it might be because you do not understand the potential of a penny doubling over time. By only day 25, you will have taken home $650,116.81 in pay! When applied to your personal growth, or to your earning power, allowing yourself to improve one percent at a time has the same potential.

Be willing to change one percent at a time. When you are sixty-five percent over the traumas of the past the remaining thirty-five percent will likely disappear without even giving you notice. As your ability to forgive and forget grows, your internal sense of benevolent personal power will also grow. It all starts with one percent. Benevolent power - the ability to be true to yourself and respectful of others no matter what the circumstances - is ultimately more rewarding than the caustic power of anger, hate, resentment, and bitterness.

The Payoff to Not Forgive and Forget

Resentment is one of those holes in the fabric of our being. When we remember every infraction we continually create new soul-holes. What happens when we stretch and tear at our soul so much that it cannot bear one more hurt? Some people believe this is when physical illness occurs.

This is exemplified in the movie *A Thousand Acres*, which explores the generational effect of harboring resentment and anger. It is about a farmer who leaves his farm to his two daughters. After their mother died when they were very young, the father practiced every kind of abuse imaginable on his daughters. Later in life, the father showed no remorse for the damage inflicted on his children and continued with verbal abuse until he died. The sister who was most angry and resentful died of cancer. With her last few breaths she tried to list her accomplishments in life. On the top of her list of accomplishments was this statement, "I did not forgive the unforgivable. That must count for something."

It is not easy to forgive or forget those who do not accept responsibility, who show no remorse for wreaking havoc on another life, who seem to have no understanding of the wreckage they have strewn in the paths of others. That is why I suggest the one percent formula. If it were easy, we could forgive all in one fell swoop!

The future can never be fully embraced while holding onto the past. Become motivated to do something about a shallow future, and be determined not to allow one more shred of energy to be focused in the past. The past cannot be changed. However, you can design your future. Never quite forgetting means a life never quite lived. The future beckons but the past is not left far enough behind. It crowds the present. If we do not forgive we are destined to suffer – or die – for our aggressor. We deserve much more than that. One percent forgiveness and one percent forgetting, just for today, just one day at a time, is one answer to finding peace of mind.

As I said before in an earlier chapter, when I ask you to forgive and forget it is not as if your memory of the event(s) that inflicted pain on you will be washed away forever. It is just that when you do recall them, the memory will not have that static charge, as it were, that reactivates the hurt, sadness, anger, and resentment. Isn't getting to this stage worth working for?

THE PAY-OFF FOR FORGETTING   **THE PAY-OFF FOR RESENTMENT**

THE PAY-OFF FOR FORGETTING	THE PAY-OFF FOR RESENTMENT
Loss / Hurt	Loss / Hurt
↓	↓
Grief	Grief / Anger / Resentment
↓	↓
Painful memories / Feelings and emotions	Painful memories / Feelings and emotions
↓	↓
Resolution	No resolution
↓	↓
Freedom to begin moving on	No movement forward
	↓
	Anger toward others
	↓
	Unhappy life
	↓
	Continuous pain that causes further pain

CHAPTER XIV

FOUR TYPES OF FORGIVENESS

*T*HE PROCESS OF FORGIVENESS IS SIMPLE BUT NOT EASY. LIVING A LIFE WITHOUT FORGIVENESS IS MUCH HARDER THAN FORGIVING EVEN THE WORST OFFENDERS.

Forgiveness Is a Gift You Give to Yourself

Many health practitioners believe that our long-held feelings of bitterness, anger, and resentment contribute to poor health, extreme low energy, and poor life decisions. It is as if we had a vast supply of resources available to us but, with the ongoing effects of resentment and anger, we could only access a fraction of our potential.

Ultimately, practicing forgiveness is a gift we give to ourselves, to our family, and to those with whom we work and play. Those with a forgiving attitude find it easier to let minor aggravations pass without venting or complaining. It is not that they are not aware of this; it's just that their attention doesn't linger there.

The four kinds of forgiveness:

1. Seeking God's forgiveness
2. Forgiving others
3. Forgiving yourself
4. Seeking the forgiveness of others

The process of being forgiven and seeking the forgiveness of others can take a long time and be a challenging process with much suffering or it may be accomplished quickly with great ease. Our approach and our attitude will determine these factors.

1. Seeking God's Forgiveness

I was discussing the power of forgiveness with a close friend who was trying in vain to get an ex-boyfriend out of her mind. She said, "I couldn't ask God to forgive Scott for all the terrible things he did to me because I wouldn't mean it and, therefore, I would feel phoney." This is a natural feeling but remember; knowing how to forgive but choosing not to is sentencing yourself to a lifetime of emotional pain.

I asked if she would be willing to have an honest conversation with God about her need to forgive this person from the past. She thought for a moment and said that she would, but that her request would not be sweetness and light. Instead, it would be full of the anger that she was feeling. In other words, she wanted to be emotionally congruent where her words matched her true emotions.

We agreed she had nothing to lose. Her prayer went something like this, "God, you know I do not mean it, but would you forgive this slime-sucking, useless, fraudulent person? I would really like Scott to burn in hell forever, but I am told the only way to get rid of obsessing about him is to forgive him. Well, I cannot, so I am handing this over to you."

She agreed to make this request and to do her daily one percent for ten days. Four months later during one of our telephone conversations I asked her how her strategy to forgive was working. She laughed and said not only were her angry, resentful memories receding, but she was also feeling closer to God. I was confused until she explained that before her request, she had thought she should only go to God with a countenance full of goodness.

The resentment and anger in her heart caused her to feel spiritually undeserving. In this instance, a pure intention with harsh words was more effective than not making the prayer at all. As another bonus, she had not thought of Scott, much less obsessed about him, for weeks. She did not remember when he had slipped away from her thoughts and memories. His absence created a vacuum in her mind and if there is one thing the universe cannot stand, it is a vacuum. In this case, the space was filled with peace of mind.

Shortly after releasing her negative emotions the depression that had plagued my friend for years began to lift. As she discovered, forgiving the person who hurt her was a gift she gave herself.

Becoming a forgiving person is not a process for the faint of heart. It requires courage. In fact, asking for help and being willing to be influenced by others who have what we want is a sign of emotional wellness, a release of emotional isolation. Fear, doubt, and insecurity are the by-products of emotional and spiritual isolation. Asking for help ends the isolation. We can enlist help from God, or from our own version of a Higher Power, before we come to a place of forgiveness.

2. Forgiving Others

Consider the possibility that when people either deliberately or unconsciously hurt us, they steal our innocence and leave us their fear. This fear manifests in us as:

- Resentment
- Inability to manage our emotions and feelings
- Frozen feelings
- Judgment of ourselves and others
- Inability to initiate or face confrontation

When we carry the burden of these consequences we are in bondage to the perpetrator. This depletes us of vital energy, leads to dissatisfaction, and gives us an overall sense of disappointment in life. The answer is to find the higher story, to find a beneficial lesson in everything negative that happens to us. When we do, we do not get lost in bondage to others because we place some value on the experience. We feel some gratitude to the perpetrator. There are three steps to finding this higher story, to finding the place in ourselves where we are able to forgive others:

Step #1: Release Your Emotions

Become well and truly fed up with yourself for thinking about the very person you do not want to think about. Long for freedom of thought and a release of emotions. Know that to resent someone is to pour a cup of poison for your perpetrator only to drink it yourself!

Step #2: Know the Behaviors of Fear

Select the attributes of the person who hurt you. Refer to the list of behaviors on the left side of the table on page 50 (Chapter 8) under the heading of Fear. Check off those behaviors you attribute to the person who hurt you. Next, imagine what it must be like for this person, the object of your anger and resentment, to go through life with these character traits.

Step #3: Feel One Percent Compassion

This is the most important step. Be willing to feel compassion for people who live most of their lives coming from a place of fear. Imagine not knowing the special bonding that comes from consistently giving and receiving love. Compassion is the key to releasing resentment and forgiving others. You might think, "It's so sad that my father/spouse/friend/co-worker/lover/mother has gone through life only knowing fear." Remember Christ's prayer, "Father, forgive them for they know not what they do."

As thoughts of the old injury arise, immediately think to yourself, "It is so sad that he/she was stuck in, and operating from, fear." That is a compassionate thought and compassion is the seed of forgiveness. For today, all you need is one percent compassion. When you reach sixty-five percent of forgiveness you have reached a critical mass, and finally you will be free. You will have claimed back your innocence – an open heart, ready to be hurt again.

If you are hurt again, you may again feel resentment. The blessed change in your life, however, is that now you have a simple process to take you out of resentment. You can release in hours or days what used to take weeks or months. Although the risk of having an open heart is vulnerability, the choice to be hard-hearted is to cut yourself off from the rewards of life.

You must go through a process of forgiveness – if not for an issue you are currently facing, then one from your past. If you do not go through this process you are also exhibiting emotions and behaviors that come from the fear column in the table on page 50 (Chapter 8), just like your perpetrators. If you do not release the harsh feelings, fear will have co-opted you into its game plan which is to make sure that you have a bitter life, that you do not reach your potential.

Living with fear but without the balancing effects of courage is not the way life is meant to be. We are meant to challenge fear so that fear does not own us. In doing so, we become stronger for having had fear in our lives. We can never get rid of fear. The best we can do is outfox it. Now is the time to outfox fear once and for all!

Hard-heartedness knows no love, no joy, and no compassion. Sure, a hard heart cannot be broken as easily because it stops us from experiencing a wide range of life. However, a hard heart is a depressed heart even if you are coping with the responsibilities of living rather well. It means that instead of taking life on life's terms, you are using energy to try to make life meet you on your terms.

Think of a full piano keyboard with eighty-eight keys. A hard heart finds a narrower range and plays only those keys. Whichever range you are stuck in is the range in which you are emotionally starved, even if you are playing the high notes. In reality, the forgiveness you must feel is not for another. It is for you. Open your heart. Yes, open yourself to being hurt again and experience a full life – all eighty-eight keys.

Forgiveness helps you purchase peace of mind. There is no amount of money that can equal the gift of a still mind.

3. Forgiving Yourself

Again, review the table on page 50 noticing where you fit in both columns. Now that you have completed an inventory of the person who hurt you and have gone on to feel compassion and forgiveness, go through the same process for yourself. Ask yourself some "call to truth" questions about your character and behavior, such as:

1. Am I resentful? Is it easy and safe for others to discuss issues and concerns with me, or do I become defensive and retaliate?

2. Do I criticize and find fault, or do I reassure others that they are doing the best they can?

3. Am I willing to listen to others' opinions with an open mind, looking for greater understanding of them, or do I want to prove

to them that they are wrong and that my opinion is right for them?

4.   Am I willing to gossip about others, or do I actively say, "Sorry, I can only say critical things about someone if that person is actually in the room."

The last point describes a true act of courage! Gossiping about another is just a form of cheap bonding. If a person comes to you with gossip about someone, know for sure that given the smallest opportunity this person will choose to gossip about you.

No matter what we discover in our self-analysis, it is important to forgive ourselves. We did the best we could at the time with what we knew, based on the circumstances in which we found ourselves. There is no value in not forgiving ourselves, although guilt, which is another form of fear, would tell us otherwise. Fear tries to convince us that we are undeserving of compassion and forgiveness, but everyone is worthy of peace of mind.

One of our negative self-talk statements might be, "With all I have going for me, why haven't I amounted to more than this?" It is good to look at our fears, weaknesses, limitations, and forgive them. Do not be discouraged. Weaknesses are character strengths that are waiting to be transformed. For instance, a person who acts as a busybody, constantly monitoring the behavior of others, might have an underlying need for justice and fair play. This need for justice and fair play, taken to the extreme, can manifest itself as control freak behavior.

One of the fastest ways to have joy show on our face is to release the resentment we have toward others. To forgive them is to give ourselves the gift of freedom. The natural outcome of forgiving others is that we become more forgiving of ourselves. Forgiveness is the best face-lift we can give ourselves.

No one responds perfectly to others or to themselves. As we begin to forgive others for being flawed humans, we can begin to forgive ourselves for being imperfect. We are human beings, not human doings. A 'human doing' might be able to do life perfectly, but as human beings, we must accept the shortcomings of others and of ourselves. Who among us has not made mistakes? The old saying is true: To err is human, to forgive divine.

In fact, as I work with others to help prepare them to be highly functioning team members, **I show them the twenty-five percent chart.** That is to say, twenty-five percent of you, over time, will annoy me. Conversely, twenty-five percent of me will irritate you. Therefore, when either of us is inclined to complain about or resent the other, it diffuses the negative energy to say, "It's only the twenty-five percent of you that upsets me. I bet my twenty-five percent has you choked right now, too. I will let this irritation go for now by asking myself, 'How important is getting immersed in this resentment or frustration today?'

Think of the twenty-five percent as personality and the remaining seventy-five percent as character. As we become attracted or repelled by the twenty-five percent, we miss learning about the other person's character and the principles by which that person lives. Some people say you must forgive yourself before you can forgive others. This belief is similar to the pre-flight instructions we are given before the airplane takes off. In the event of an emergency, the flight attendant instructs, we should place the oxygen mask over our own face first. Only when ours is firmly secured should we help others with their oxygen masks. Frequently, this sequence works for forgiveness as well; we need to forgive ourselves first, before forgiving others and lead us out of the resentment and judging trap.

However, the reverse was true for me. I needed to forgive others before I could turn my full attention to forgiving myself. In fact, it became evident that I needed to make far more amends to myself than I did to anyone else. I seem to have expected much more from myself than I have expected from the others around me. This inability to take care of myself was a result of not knowing how to create elegant boundaries. The consequence of that was feeling obliged to do more and give more than my fare share.

When I became tired and exhausted from doing more than my fair share, you guesses it…I became resentful!

4. Seeking the Forgiveness of Others

Asking others to forgive the wrongs we have done to them may be the most difficult form of forgiveness to practice.

The other three forms of forgiveness are mainly an internal job. But asking others for forgiveness makes us feel vulnerable because we are admitting our imperfections, exposing our weaknesses and our desires. Being willing to do this, despite our trepidation, is by itself a measure of our inner growth.

As we go through life we are sure to inflict pain and suffering onto others. It is my belief that only a small percentage of people deliberately want to hurt others. Whether we hurt others by design or by default, we can play a large role in helping them recover their sense of balance. Only the strongest people are able to detach from the emotion of being hurt and refuse to take the infraction personally. Usually, when we hurt others they need to hear us express remorse and ask for forgiveness, even if they appear to be able to let the infraction go. When a hurt occurs, trust is broken.

Hearing, "I'm sorry," or "I apologize," does help. However, going the distance and asking for forgiveness takes the focus from the wrongdoer and places it on the wronged person. There are five benefits to saying, "I'm sorry, please forgive me."

1. It helps the person who has been harmed feel validated in their feelings.
2. It creates a space for the relationship to improve. A person who is accountable for their insensitive behavior is perceived as more trustworthy.
3. It helps the person harmed to move forward and avoid becoming stuck in the anger of the past.

4. Since apologizing is a humbling experience, it may be a deterrent to further infractions.

5. Amended behavior over a prolonged period will rebuild trust.

It is not only the words we say but also how we say them that counts. Demanding an apology or asking someone else to apologize might inflame a situation because *a person convinced against his or her will to apologize is still not remorseful.*

A reluctant or insincere apology actually worsens a situation by adding insult to injury. The one who forgives may feel appeased, but will feel even more betrayed when the nasty behavior continues. Unfortunately, insincere people often see no reason to change their behavior. Too many people accept apology after apology, but continue to tolerate intolerable behavior. An apology without changed behavior is insincere, no matter how tearfully and contritely presented. It is important to remember that there are two types of amends, verbal amends and living amends.

Verbal amends acknowledge the infraction and express remorse. Living amends become part of one's lifestyle – the person does not practice that behavior again. They express remorse and by their behavior, they demonstrate this remorse to be authentic and worthy of continued trust. In reality, their words and their actions match.

Asking Others to Forgive Us: Six Steps to Making Amends

Let's face it, relationships are difficult. Most small day-to-day infractions are easily forgiven and forgotten. But what do we do when we are the perpetrators, when we make a mistake and deeply offend or wound? Assume you have blundered and deeply offended someone. Now you want to make things right. There is a six-step process for this, a process I sometimes call Mess Up and Fess Up!

Step #1: Name It and Claim It

Admit one hundred percent responsibility for the infraction. Thinking to yourself, "I wouldn't have done it if she hadn't been so mean to me first," does not serve you one bit. The extent that you hold anyone or any circumstance responsible for your words, feelings or actions is the extent to which the outside world has control over you. Remember that self-government and self-management are states that human beings strive for and yet at the same time, resist. These states cannot be achieved without great stock-taking and personal inventory on your part.

You might say, "Janis, last week I did something for which I am not proud. This is what I did, and I want you to know that I know I was wrong."

Step #2: Express Empathy

Put yourself in the other person's shoes. Although easier said than done, <u>it is vital to put words to the wrong you have committed.</u> This lets the other person know that you know the source of the pain caused. You could ask yourself, "What would I be feeling or thinking if this happened to me?" In a non-judgmental manner, express this sentiment to the one you hurt. For instance, you might say one, some, or all of the following:

- I imagine you must feel betrayed?
- My sense is you feel disappointed and confused by my behavior?
- I would feel upset and disrespected if I were you. Is this how you feel?
- I imagine you are thinking that I do not care?

Notice that these thoughts are expressed as questions or even suggestions instead of absolutes. No one wants to be told how he or she is feeling. Doing so would represent a judgment. Scanning the situation and checking your perceived reality is discernment. Be aware of the difference a small change will make.

Step #3: Make a Semi-Rash Promise

A rash promise is to say, "I promise this will never happen again. I promise never again to do anything to hurt your feelings." This is nearly impossible since we are imperfect people with complicated relationships in an imperfect world. It is more beneficial to say, "I'm going to do the best I can to be conscious of not hurting or offending you again."

You must always come from the highest intention. Don't just follow the process because you know it will disarm your victim and pave the way for you to make the same mistake again. It is important to scan and cleanse your intentions, to constantly search for any hidden agendas. And when you find hidden agendas, uncover them and take corrective action.

Step #4: Give the One You Hurt the Greatest Gift of All

You must provide an opportunity for the one you hurt to express forgiveness. Yes, directly and humbly ask for forgiveness. You do not need to be on your knees begging but you do need to ask.

Saying, "I'm sorry," or "I apologize," is not enough because it is still all about you! Any sentence that begins with the first-person pronoun ("I") is all about you. The person you offended or hurt needs to hear you acknowledge your infractions. When you blithely say, "I'm sorry," or "I apologize for what happened last week," you are being self-centered and letting yourself off the hook. Most people will feel obligated to say, "Oh, that's okay." But resolution has not occurred and trust and respect has not even begun to be recreated. Getting back to trust is the goal of making amends. You could say:

- Are you able to forgive someone with an attitude like mine?
- Do you think you can ever forgive me for hurting you?
- I realize that I broke your trust, but I want you to know that I want a relationship with you. Would you be willing to begin to forgive me?

Most people are willing to forgive if they sense your sincerity. When trust is regained the relationship is usually better than before. Why? I can only postulate that as a relationship progresses through difficulties, honest appraisal and integrity are established and it becomes reliable. We show that we are bigger than the problems and the embarrassing moments. As heat and hard knocks temper steel so too, it seems, are relationships – as long as we stay in respectful communication.

However, the process of making amends may be stymied because the other person may choose not to forgive. This is unfortunate. The other person cannot help it. Resentment, anger, and righteousness may fuel them. Most people, when they know the benefits and the simple steps are willing to begin to forgive, one percent at a time.

For those who do not agree to forgive you, you can practice what I call courageous vulnerability where you open yourself up by asking for forgiveness, knowing that you may be repeatedly rejected. Asking directly for forgiveness completes the circle in terms of your responsibility. This does not prevent you from re-opening the issue by asking again. Each time you ask for forgiveness you enter into a spiritual moment!

One way to see courageous vulnerability in action is to visit a dog-walking park. Watch what happens when young puppies approach older dogs. The first thing they do is lie on their backs, paws folded, and inviting attack. What they are effectively communicating is this, "I know you have the ability to hurt me. I'm offering you my soft underbelly (as we offer up our feelings to one another) knowing that you, big dog, can end my life with one snap of your jaws!"

This courage is not available to many of us because our defenses come to the forefront and rob us of those strengthening, growing experiences. Our egos seem to say, "Don't admit anything. Blame it on them. Carry on louder and longer than they do." Some perpetrators even posture and act as offended as their victims, and some victims may begin to believe they somehow contributed to their own abuse.

Take the example of a friend constantly giving unsolicited advice. When you finally create a boundary by asking the friend to end this practice, the friend may become annoyed saying, "I go out of my way to help you, and this is how you show your gratitude!" In such cases, a sense of humor and a strong sense of ourselves can go a long way.

People often ask me to coach them on the process of forgiving a perpetrator. I strongly recommend that they ask for forgiveness at least three times. If the answer is still no, then let the other person go with my favorite blessing: *God bless them, improve me.* Those who don't want to forgive need resentment to fuel them, so if it wasn't you they would find someone else to cause them grief.

Ask for forgiveness at least three times, knowing that you will always get most of what you ask for, and you will miss one hundred percent of what you do not ask for. Also, remember that you are not entitled to forgiveness just because you ask. You need to stop the offending behavior. That is a living amendment.

Step #5: How Can I Make It Up to You?

If you have moved on to the fifth step, you are lucky. The person has either agreed to begin to forgive you or has forgiven you entirely. Respond to their forgiveness by sincerely asking, "What can I do to make it up to you?" If the forgiveness has begun the usual response will be, "That's okay, forget it." You do not have to do anything. However, that is from their point of view. From yours, you must do two things. One, do not repeat the offending action. Two, do something nice anyway. This is where chocolates and flowers come in!

Step #6: Re-Open the Can of Worms

Relationship rebuilding is in progress and a few weeks have gone by. Now it is time for you to re-visit the issue to check if your relationship is still on track. This step may sound mechanical and systematic, but it is not. You must make a conscious effort because you are creating a relationship by design instead of by default.

At this point, many people balk and ask, "Why re-open old wounds?" The reason is that if the wound is festering, it is better to know now so you can take corrective action. If all is well, there is no risk, is there? This simple yet courageous step will enhance the relationship. It shows once again how much you care. The other person will likely feel even more valued and wanted. He or she sees you visibly doing the work, showing up for both of you in a connected, and trusting relationship.

Recently, a single friend lamented about not being able to meet her match. I suggested connecting her with a friend of mine but she declined. He asked me for her number anyway, and thinking I knew what was best for her I gave it to him, contrary to her wishes. I see now how disrespectful this was, and she told me so directly. I used the six-step process for making amends and after three weeks, with great trepidation, I brought the subject up again by asking if she had any lingering concerns, but she balanced this one act of poor judgment on my part with how good a friend I had been over the years. She reassured me that she had moved on and totally forgiven me. I will never do such a thing again, to her or to anyone else.

Of course you will feel uncomfortable when asking for forgiveness but always remember, no fear means no courage. The moment you take action, even imperfect fumbling, or uncomfortable action in the midst of fear, you turn it from a dark force paralyzing you into something spiritual, good, and true. It will light your way to wonderful relationships in which you are loved and in which you flourish, imperfect as you are.

CHAPTER XV

THE SAD VICTIM

*H*OW WOULD YOU FEEL IF YOU WERE
THE VICTIM, THE ONE WHO HAD BEEN HURT?
LIKELY, YOU WOULD FEEL BETRAYED AND
DISAPPOINTED.

The Victim's Point Of View

It would be wise to avoid wearing these despairing feelings as a position from which to gain martyrdom, sympathy, and attention. Some people claim the mantle of victimhood to get attention from others, and to gain evidence of their caring, support, and loyalty.

Your feelings of betrayal will begin to recede if the person who hurt you is accountable, takes responsibility for prior actions and demonstrates a desire to be trusted again. But you cannot count on others being remorseful about their treatment of you.

When people are mean, nasty or disrespectful, it is a reflection of the way they feel about themselves. It is impossible to project gestures of love, generosity, and gratitude toward others if these attributes are not part of one's character. When people are critical of others they are declaring to the world who and what they are inside. When people criticize us we can create a personal shield to mitigate the hurt feelings by saying, "This hurts. This really hurts. I feel horrified that I've experienced this, but this is not about me and I will not let it ruin my day or my life!"

It also helps to remember that the container of who we are can only express its true contents. If our container is filled with love, generosity and acceptance, these are the sentiments we will express. Conversely, if our container is filled with hate, self-loathing and aggression, these will be expressed. This supports the old adage, "Think before you speak." What you say declares who you are.

Self-Forgiveness at Last

Before going to bed one night I was writing in my journal that I wanted to become more diligent with my exercise program and as I slept my dream guides decided to hold a personal growth seminar in my subconscious. I dreamed that I had to remember back as far as possible and list every mistake I had committed. Otherwise, any program I undertook would yield poor results.

Although I recognized this as good advice upon awakening, I did not heed it immediately. However, I finally had to take action because my attention was scattered all over the landscape, and my focus on work and deadlines was non-existent. I did the spiritual work of listing the litany of mistakes I felt sure I had made throughout my life. The formula that evolved (yes, another prescription) was quite a wonderful gift.

I drew a line down the middle of a page and listed my mistakes on the left side, beginning with the earliest year I could remember. On the right side, I listed the lessons and opportunities that resulted from the mistake. In other words, I told myself a higher story about each incident. I proceeded in five-year time periods. In listing the mistakes, I did not create drama or remember any emotional pain. I was simply on assignment from my higher self.

By the end of the exercise I began to wish I had made more mistakes in my life. The recognition of opportunities and lessons that arose from those mistakes was nothing less than amazing. What I thought would be painful was very inspiring. I plan to go back over the list on occasion and see if my perception of the mistakes has changed. The following worksheet may help you plan your own discoveries.

Prescription for Self-Forgiveness:

Date of mistake: _____

Mistake / failure: _____

Lesson / opportunity: _____

I used/will use this lesson to: _____

Date of mistake: _____

Mistake / failure: _____

Lesson / opportunity: _____

I used/will use this lesson to: _____

A weakness is a strength taken to the extreme.

Because of my nightly schedule of self-assessment, and regular doses of compassion, I am able to notice my weaknesses in a lovingly detached manner and then develop a plan to transform those weaknesses, over time, into strengths. As I said before, when treated with compassion I often discover that a weakness is only a strength taken to the extreme. For instance, stubbornness is often considered a weakness because it seems a stubborn person is unwilling to enter a conversation with open-mindedness. The intention is often only to point out to the other person that he or she is wrong. However, the positive virtue of stubbornness is determination, and who among us could not use a stronger dose of determination from time to time?

If, in moments of self-assessment, I notice I have caused hurt or injury to another, I go through the process of asking for forgiveness and making amends. This may look like a spiritual quality to outsiders but for me, it is self-serving. When I have disrespected another person, I feel bad. I feel shame and guilt in healthy doses.

You might think that having written this book on forgiveness and for being an avid Forgiveness Practitioner that I would not mess up but that is not so. Sometimes my emotions get the best of me. Just last week, I became angry with a customer service person at the cell phone store. I raised my voice and explained that I was in need of customer service now and that clearly she was lacking those skills...then I marched out. I thought that I could forget the incident but my peace of mind was compromised and I knew that there would eventually be untoward consequences, such as watching too much TV or becoming tired and exhausted for a few days. I wished that I could go back in time and take my words and my uppity attitude back, but I could not. It was when I began to fret that my conduct was in some way harming her, I went into action and bought a Starbuck's gift card and walked back into the store and apologized. Interestingly, when I had practiced the outburst, no one was in the store and when I apologized and gave her the gift card, I had a large audience. Naturally, as most people would in a similar situation, she was gracious and accepting. When I think about that incident now it is with regret but not with shame. Before apologizing to her, I felt both guilt and shame. Now she does not carry me on her back and I do not carry her on mine!

Shame and guilt are healthy, however, if they propel us to change our behavior from fear to peace of mind. The extent to which I feel shame and guilt is the extent to which my peace of mind is disturbed, and I am a junkie for a clear conscience and for peace of mind! Consequently, I am vigilant about behaving towards others in keeping with the behaviors listed in the Peace of Mind column from the table on page 50 (Chapter 8).

What I give, ultimately I receive. I give someone compassion and forgiveness, and I get peace of mind. I give someone the opportunity to extend forgiveness to me, and once again, I receive peace of mind. If I am a forgiving person, I can reasonably expect to be forgiven by others, by myself and by God whose forgiveness I believe is unconditional!

When the correlation between making mistakes and learning a lesson or discovering an opportunity is clear, forgiving me for my humanity becomes much easier. I offer this prescription to you hoping that your peace of mind will increase because of my work! Should you try this exercise and not be able to forgive yourself, put the exercise aside for a few days and return to it with a rested and refreshed mind. Another option is to ask the universe for your own unique path to self-forgiveness. The answers that before were unclear may now become glaringly obvious.

Unmet Expectations

The expression *damned by faint praise* carries a lot of weight. Some of the most hurtful acts are not what was done, but *what was never done* for us. Withheld compliments, acknowledgment, or recognition of our achievements can do as much damage as a physical blow.

As children, we looked to our parents for acknowledgement. I grew up in a time when pride in oneself was considered a sin. "Pride goes before a fall," and "If you get too big in yourself, someone will have to take you down to size," were both common expressions used to withhold acknowledgement. That silence in the face of eagerly anticipated recognition cut deeper than a knife. Eventually, children in these situations toughen up and not being acknowledged becomes normal.

Children who grow up receiving messages like those quickly learn not to solicit recognition actively at home. Nevertheless, it is still an unfulfilled need so they seek to have it met elsewhere. The lucky ones find it by excelling at school and gaining a teacher's recognition. The unfortunate ones seek recognition from destructive sources. In most cases, love or expressions of love were not withheld as deliberate acts of meanness. Instead, it was because the caretakers were incapable of doing any more. Caretakers who are filled with insecurities and fear cannot consistently demonstrate love and kindness. Few people can overcome the results of emotional deprivation unless they do the hard work of scanning and releasing their defenses.

One of the symptoms of growing up in an environment of conditional love is the fear of not being worthy to receive that which we need, so we make do with whatever shows up. Our radar or early warning system for incompatibility is seriously warped. We fear the withholder somehow has an insight into us, has taken a deep look at the essence of who it is that we are and has found us wanting. Then the chase is on. We redouble our efforts, thinking, "Maybe now my current success will cause my loved ones to recognize my worthiness. Maybe now I will finally receive the recognition I deserve." Of course, a withholder is a withholder and the cycle ramps up. In other words, our people picker is warped. What I mean by that statement is that somehow those of us who grew up in a conditional, critical, chaotic environment consistently pick people who continue to create the same scenarios. As Ernest Hemmingway said, "The world breaks all of us; some become stronger at the broken places." Those who become stronger learn to go within for the requisite recognition and self-care and eventually live a good life.

Imagine a child going to a well with a bucket in each hand. We tell the child that the well is empty. However, the need is so great that the child thinks, *I will try just once more.* And history repeats itself, especially is he or she receives a tiny bit of love or recognition. The only answer not to be hurt by the lack of recognition or acknowledgment is to not need it in the first place. Easier said than done.

Little Children Have Little Hearts.

Imagine the same child achieving an award in school, sharing the good news with family and friends and wanting but not needing anyone to approve. The child is happy inside with his or her accomplishment. Having others give positive feedback is simply icing on the cake. Sadly, this emotional maturity and equanimity usually occurs only with age. By that stage, we have activated a host of defenses to soothe our hungry hearts.

It often requires decades to be able to detach externally from the withholding behavior of others. I am not suggesting that you need to detach from anyone who you feel does not give credit where credit is due. Rather, forgive and accept them for who they are, and for who they are not. You may also discover your own role in withholding. Ask yourself these questions:

1. Have there been occasions when someone came to me hoping for acknowledgment and I deliberately withheld encouragement?
2. Do I generally find it difficult to give encouragement to others? If so, why is that? Is it because to acknowledge the good in others is to say less about me?

3. Do I love to receive positive feedback but find it difficult to give the same feedback to others?

4. If someone looks smart do I feel his or her success makes me look small?

5. Do I look at the success of other people and ask myself how they do that? What is so special about them, and not so special about me?

Giving others feedback is like putting money in the bank. When deposits are made daily, they shore up the relationship. Some partners say "I love you" several times a day. To someone visiting from another planet this behavior might seem odd. The visitor might think, *these earthlings have short memories. They forget that their partner loves them. They need constant reminding of their partner's love.*

In fact, saying those three little words helps maintain commitment and bonding. The consistent deposits are there for the occasions when we act less than loving and make withdrawals. Because of the daily deposits we can make occasional withdrawals without fear of losing the connection. If more withdrawals are made than deposits, the relationship suffers and serious repairs are necessary to get back to love and respect.

It is important for all of us to look for reasons to validate the people who are important to us. Validation and feedback are like mortar holding the bricks together.

Unstated Expectations

Having expectations of others that cannot/will not be met is asking to be hurt first and then resentful later. Resentment builds when we have expectations of others that we have not confirmed as being realistic. Any expectation that has not been validated is a hallucination. It is something we made up without checking out our assumptions.

Cathy's boyfriend, David, asked her to marry him. After a few months of being engaged he declared that he wanted to support her in her career by being her stay-at-home partner. In his words, he wanted to be the wind beneath her wings.

Cathy thought about the offer and realized David was often disappointed because she did not recognize all that he did for her. After a long discussion with him, she realized David felt he gave her twenty gallons of support a day. However, she only needed three gallons of support on any given day. As a result, she only recognized and expressed three gallons of gratitude.

Consequently, David felt under-appreciated. He became resentful toward Cathy for not giving him what he needed – gratitude on par with his perceived level of giving. In the midst of all that support, there was David in the center, feeling nicer, kinder, and superior to his partner.

The net result was seventeen gallons of resentment on his part which amounts to *tyranny of the nice*. Simply put, if someone gives and gives and gives but does not receive gratitude or favors in return, his or her niceness may be clouding deep resentment. Therein lies the tyranny of the nice.

David was busy being generous but he expected an equal measure of gratitude must be returned. This expectation was not communicated. All of that niceness had a price.

Happily, for Cathy, she was finally able to free herself from taking responsibility and doing for others what they could do for themselves. In the 1980's and 1990's those who stepped in to rescue others were finally diagnosed as co-dependent. This is one of the most difficult diseases from which to recover. After all, the co-dependent is convinced imminent danger is just around the corner and the only way to ensure personal, emotional, or physical safety is to be all things to all people.

Confounding this disease is the ready supply of people wanting to be on the receiving end of all of that giving.

I have often wondered why those who kept on taking, enjoying the good life at the cost of another, had no books written for them! One supposes that living the good life is not something from which a person would want to recover.

Chapter XVI

GIVING AND RECEIVING

A RESPONSIBILITY GOES WITH BOTH RECEIVING AND GIVING. THE RESPONSIBILITY OF A GIVER IS EITHER TO GIVE WITHOUT EXPECTATIONS OR TO NEGOTIATE FOR RECIPROCITY. THE RECEIVER MUST LOOK FOR AN OPPORTUNITY TO RETURN THE FAVOR.

The Victim's Point Of View

The giver may clearly contract for payment or reciprocity. The responsibility of the receiver is not to be a taker without asking about what is required in return. Giving back in a meaningful way to those who give to us is reciprocity. When there is no reciprocity, the generous flow ends or the giver becomes a martyr. If we are going to give to another, it needs to be either unconditional or negotiated. If I help you move to your new apartment at the end of the month, am I to assume I can call on you for a similar favor when the time comes? It is perfectly reasonable to have expectations of others. However, unless we check them out those expectations are tantamount to hallucinations.

When we have an expectation that another person will do or say something, clearly communicate that expectation. You may not like what you hear but at least you will be living the truth instead of flailing around in an illusion. Most disagreements arise from a perceived broken agreement, an unmet expectation. When we are clear that what we need is not forthcoming, we must make two choices — to engage in clear communication about your expectations, realistically determine which are going to be met, decide whether or not to accept reality and then determine to stay in the relationship, or not. It is a delicate balance to maintain. Asking for, and expecting to have our needs met all of the time is quite a burden to place on another.

My mother had a great rule that she passed on to me: asking for what you want more than three times is nagging. At that point, you are crossing over to the dark side, so you had better find a way to do it yourself! The gift in this piece of advice is that you can become competent and resilient and your validation can come primarily from inside. Otherwise, you can become resentful and angry, which leads to dismantling your peace of mind. We can learn to avoid being like that little child going to the empty well. We can come to know the well is empty but we are full inside. Christ asked us to forgive those who cannot, or will not, be generous in their actions, emotions, and words of acknowledgment, for they know not what they do.

Most Disappointments Arise from Unmet Expectations

When those close to us refuse to acknowledge us, it becomes imperative that we acknowledge ourselves. In fact, their refusing to acknowledge us may be a gift. Because of our sadness we shift from seeking outside acknowledgment and begin to develop our own inner appreciation of ourselves. When we begin to do this for ourselves, we heal. Rather than waiting for the mythical prince or princess to show up, our neediness lessens. Sometimes, it seems that the purpose of adulthood is to recover from childhood!

Big Questions Yield Big Answers

When we are willing to ask ourselves big questions, with the pure intention of truly understanding and accepting what we learn, we get big answers. The biggest questions of all begin with this phrase:

What is it about me that:
- Cannot let go of the person who hurt(s) me?
- Makes others eager to help me?
- Lets me have a happy, supportive relationship?
- Makes me unfazed by drama around me?
- Allows me to tolerate the intolerable?
- Causes business to flow my way?
- Enables me to personalize feedback?
- Makes me want what I want rather than taking life on life's terms?
- Gives me energy to spare?
- Causes me to stay around people who disrespect me?
- Makes me generally feel good about myself?
- Attracts people who disrespect me?
- Makes this person choose to be in my life?

The process of forgiveness does not mean we condone or accept the behaviors of others. It means we do not hooked by them. Think of a fish with a hook in its mouth, controlled and yanked around by an angler.

Using energy to be resentful of another is just like that hooked fish, caught on someone's line.

Give yourself the gift of forgiveness, just for today, by becoming a one percenter. You do not have to do it in one fell swoop. Each day just forgive one person by one percent. If you can forgive completely, then do so. It can happen. If you follow these processes, peace of mind will certainly develop within you, and the force of the creative and productive spirit of the universe will be yours. For each ounce of resentment housed within our core, our greater good is proportionately blocked. No one is worth this sacrifice.

Good Intentions versus Hidden Agendas

Intention is the starting point for anything worth achieving. What are your intentions around forgiving? What are your intentions around holding onto resentments?

The shadow side of an intention is the hidden agenda. Whatever you declare to be your intentions, whatever you set your compass upon, is what will show up in your life. If your hidden agenda is to get by – to get the most out of life without putting the equivalent back – you will have lackluster results.

An example of practicing good intention is to look for something good and high-spirited from the person with whom you are dealing, whether the person appears nice or cranky. It takes no courage and character to be spiritually elegant with someone who is kind, sweet, nurturing, and accommodating. However, those people who challenge our equanimity are actually gifts. They give us a chance to reach inside and find our higher strength. They give us a chance to access our accumulated resources.

Hidden agendas are generally associated with wanting to look smart at someone else's expense, to see someone else fail, to do less than others, or to get even. If you scan your intentions and hidden agendas and find a negative framework, you can know for sure that the experience of others around you were also negative. It cannot be otherwise. A consistent inventory scan of our intentions with discernment, not judgment, is the answer. This sounds simple and it is. However, it is not easy.

The first stage of the process is to accept that you are probably not aware of your hidden agendas. The best you can do is attempt to grasp the moment and to assign a feeling to the thought. You can ask yourself tough questions such as, "Could I be feeling greedy? Having experienced personal failure in one relationship, do I want to be buoyed up in another?" Maybe you feel angry and powerless in one area of your life, so you try to gain power by making someone else feel powerless.

Scanning your intentions in a discerning rather than judging way is a key method to fast forwarding personal growth and self-awareness. Very soon, you will notice the core truth of who you are. You will notice whether most of the time your thoughts are generous and helpful toward others. Or you will notice the opposite and be able to take corrective action within yourself.

Forgetting

It is not as if the sad events of your life will be erased forever. Rather, when you remember them it will be in the form of brief fleeting thoughts that have no power to hurt you.

About thirty years ago I was in divorce court. At that time, when divorce was far less common than it is today, judges actually saw the parties involved and personally officiated at the divorce sessions. The presiding judge said to one woman, "Madam is there any way you can forgive this man and take him back?"

"Judge," she replied, "I forgive him, but I never want him back."

The judge was baffled. "If you forgive him, why won't you take him back?"

"Because I will never be able to forget," she said with a sob.

Unknown to me then, I had a very smart thought, although at the time I wondered if it was a shallow one. My thought was, "Not me. If I get this divorce today, I will not spend any time thinking about the past year!"

I now know the thoughts and feelings I believed to be shallow were, in fact, smart and healthy. No resentment means more peace of mind. I accepted one hundred percent responsibility for my role, said my legal piece, and moved on. You see, the sooner we accept one hundred percent responsibility for our reactions to what happens, the sooner we move into the solution.

Therapists used to hold their clients down in the quagmire of broken childhood. They believed that reliving and rehashing painful memories was tantamount to healing. Thankfully, therapists today are moving toward fewer sessions focused on past issues with their clients. Returning repeatedly to the past keeps us stuck there. "Whatever you resist persists," and "Whatever you focus on, you get," are just two sayings that reinforce the idea of moving away from thoughts focused on past traumas.

Healthy statements to say to ourselves as we are in transition are:

1. That was then, this is now, and now is not forever.
2. I am safe, it's only change.
3. This too shall pass.

When you slip, as we all do, and find yourself ruminating about the past, you can quickly say, "I am doing the best I can for today, and that is good enough," or "Throughout my life I did the best I could, in any given stage or situation, and that's good enough." When it comes right down to it, all we can do is the best we are capable of doing in any given moment. The next example may be familiar if you have experienced the heartache of a lost love or the confusion and disappointment that comes from trusting the untrustworthy.

Instead of my ex-fiancé discussing his change of heart in person, he left me a note ending our relationship. Although he was unable to deal with his emotions (and mine) head on, he did the best he could at the time. In response, I could have layered my natural feelings of hurt and grief with anger and resentment. Instead, I worked through the stages of grief and was able to feel compassion and forgiveness just months after the loss. I realize now that he had neither the language skills nor the ability to manage his intense emotions to enable him to speak to me in person and still stand by his own truth with integrity.

In my first stages of grief it helped to repeat, "God bless him; improve me." To be honest, I also had a not so spiritual, defiant mantra, "I'll show him! I will find a way to leverage this pain!" These two sayings kept me away from the grip of anger, blame, shame, and resentment. As my friends checked in with me about this loss, they were amazed that just a couple of months later I was my usual vibrant, productive self. I still missed him and the great experiences we had shared, but a testament to the power of forgiving and forgetting was that I returned to my life in fuller measure because that loss had occurred.

It was not right or fair that I had to experience this, but clearly my partner and I did not have the ability to negotiate the issues, so we simply could not have acted differently. For me to revisit, ruminate on, and discuss this betrayal with friends would have been to wound myself again. On the rare occasions when I speak of him now, it is to remind my friends how much I learned and the gifts I received. For instance, my career has escalated because of a professional skill he taught me and this book would not have had as much significance for me without that profound forgiveness experience I extended to both him and me. You may call me shallow but I did find a way to leverage that pain!

If someone hurts you, shame on him or her. If you give that person who was disrespectful or unkind extended airtime in your thoughts and heart, shame on you.

Being free of the past

It seems that the job of our ego is to be a storehouse for the dark side of fear. Ego stands for Edging Goodness (God) Out. It seems easier to ruminate in pain and disappointment than it is to take action and change our minds. When hurts and disappointments occur, our ego takes that as an opportunity to hold us back. Fear prevents us from going forward with steps of positive action that will bring us back to a state of self-empowerment.

Just as there are steps to making amends, asking for forgiveness, telling the truth, and forgiving another person. In addition, there are five steps that will help with the forgetting process.

Step #1: Feel the Grief
Anyone who has experienced loss must go through the normal stages of grief. Grief is not just one emotion. It is actually a cascading process all rolled into one. Although the professionals (I am not qualified to be one of them) agree on the five stages of grief, I am also interested in the first two points in the list below...the betrayal and hurt that precedes the five stages of grief.

1. Betrayal
2. Hurt

Betrayal and hurt are preceded these emotions:

1. Denial
2. Anger and Resentment
3. Bargaining
4. Depression
5. Acceptance

Elizabeth Kubler-Ross has written several books on the subject of grief beginning with the book, *On Death and Dying*. Judith Viorst wrote about grief in a great book that I highly recommend, *Necessary Losses*. The late Dr. Bruce Fisher wrote the ever-popular book, *Rebuilding*, which deals with the stages of grief for those recovering from separation and divorce. The consensus of all three authors is that the most dangerous stage to be stuck in is the second stage, anger and resentment. There, the person has an understanding of the events but not a detached acceptance of them. They hearken back to the past, never quite forgetting the hurt, betrayal, embarrassment, and pain of the injury or loss.

Going through the stages of grief and coming out the other side, moving on to a fulfilled life, is the first step. Mental health professionals agree that staying stuck in the anger and resentment stage can lead to depression and despair. Yes, going through the stages of grief and feeling those feelings of loss is painful. Nevertheless, when you feel the pain and move on, the source of the pain eventually resolves and you have a peaceful life once again. If you choose to be stuck in rage or depression, you also experience painful feelings but you have nothing to show for it but a diminished life. The return on investment from resolving pain and grief is a life worth living.

Step #2: Move On

As the grief process unfolds, you must be proactive and deliberate and make a daily decision, "I will move on to the future. The present and the future are what count with me now. Just watch me grow!" Refuse to be co-opted by the very situation or person who hurt you. You can use my mantras, "I will find a way to leverage this pain" or "God bless him/her; improve me!"

Do not be embarrassed to have conversations with yourself expressing mantras that feel right for you. It may become a good habit, something you need to do to feel strong today. As Socrates said; "A life unexamined is not worth living."

Step #3: Take Back Your Power

Decide to take your own benevolent power back. Stand in its circle and deliberately use your will to replace thoughts about that hurtful situation with satisfactory thoughts about right now, even if you think about the weather! The perpetrator, the person who dumped grievousness onto you and stole your innocence, does not deserve your time and attention. If your present is clouded by the situations or the person who hurt you, your future is being compromised because now is when we prepare for the future. There is a great book called *The Power of Now: A Guide to Spiritual Enlightenment* by Eckhart Tolle. In it, Tolle examines the challenges and rewards of focusing on the present instead of the past or the future.

You can also use your anger. Let it flare up inside you and use its energy to propel you forward – but be sure to let the anger go. If you find your mind wandering to the past, say to yourself, "Bless him/her; improve me." This simple statement means you see both yourself and the perpetrator as needing help. With this thinking, you will quickly see the perpetrator as just another imperfect human being. You now are becoming strong because of the hurtful experience.

Step #4: Tell a Higher Story

The fourth way to forget is powerful. It works for any situation when people or circumstances have ruffled our sensibilities. This powerful step is to discover a higher story of what happened and then tell yourself that story. By higher story I mean, find a valuable life lesson contained in the hurtful, stressful situation. An example of finding a higher story in the midst of confusion and sadness is that my lost romance led to me writing this book. With such a positive higher story, my feelings and my entire countenance lightened. Instead of feeling hurt, I feel immense gratitude. Most days, I even suspect the universe arranged the entire experience for me so I would write this book and offer it to the world!

I hope that my ex-fiancé has found a way to achieve a positive outcome from his experience and to create something wonderful to offer to the world because of knowing me! If I can create a higher story from my troubles, he can from his and you can from yours.

Step #5: Learn from the Experience

Use the experience to learn what not to do. For instance, as a child I was obsessed with getting high marks, so much so that it took me years to see myself as a person with other than educational needs. My two strongest memories are of chewing my nails and of praying, "Please God let me get an A on this exam and I promise to study harder for the next one!"

As an aside, it has since become clear to me that I did not pass on this legacy to my own child. Instead, I made sure to let my son know that his worthiness as a human being was not contingent on the marks he received on his exams!

Healing the hole in our souls

An old African story states that if a child is hurt and criticized, his soul leaves his body and goes to another village to live. Then, as the child grows to maturity, there is restlessness and longing to fill the empty space where the soul used to be.

Lately, we often hear pop psychologists and self-help gurus refer to this idea of healing the hole in our souls but I believe our soul or spirit is whole. However, the ego has established defenses and preferences designed to create the illusion that vengeance and resentment will protect us from experiencing further pain. The point is, as children we were easily injured. Often, those who were severely hurt, those whose souls are so sad, go on to injure others. ***Hurt people hurt people.***

When we are hurt, it is easy to point a finger and identify the culprit and their offending behavior. Unfortunately, it is not as easy to turn the finger toward ourselves, to conduct an objective inventory of our own shortcomings and our transgressions toward others. Understanding that our own weaknesses are similar to the weaknesses of those whom we criticize helps us to move on, forget the past, and build a future by design instead of by default.

With all the injuries we experience throughout life our courage must eventually come to resemble Swiss cheese, with holes all over. But contained within us are also the strong parts and those strong parts are what keep us searching for a solution to resolve the hurts and to build a better life for our loved ones and for ourselves.

My 26-year-old son recently lent his car to a friend and the friend had an accident. During our discussion, he admitted as if it were a failing (though certainly it is not), that he does not have a mean streak. Consequently, he often trusts that everything will work out. In this case, he did not feel he could ensure the safety of his car and keep the friendship. In his world, buddies look out for each other, and he lent him the car.

I was happy to reassure him that it is better to have disappointments such as a dented car, than go through life believing he needs a mean streak to survive. When your general orientation is that life is safe your experience is more creative, more loving, and you enjoy greater peace of mind. Peace of mind is the greatest gift of all, and it cannot be purchased by fame or fortune. It can be gained by having a forgiving, grateful, and accepting attitude.

There is nothing wrong with valuing reciprocity. In a perfect world, the even flow of giving and receiving would occur naturally. But in this world, sometimes one person is way ahead of the other person in the friendship.

Recently I went to a pub with a few salespeople I had been coaching to celebrate a big sale. Interestingly, Bryan immediately began to tease Steve that he, Bryan, had brought a calculator to keep track of who paid for what drinks and so he (Steve) would not be able to drink more than his fair share. The banter went back and forth but it was clear that Bryan was sending a very serious message…Steve's freeloading ways were about to end.

If you were to draw four concentric circles, the inner most being A surrounded by B, C, and D, would you put a freeloader in the coveted A position? Would you be considered an A-list friend if you received without reciprocating? You may not have considered your behaviors around giving and receiving like this before. Just because you are unaware of the impact of your taking, without reciprocating, has on your friends does not mean they are oblivious to the situation.

Would it be wrong to find an elegant way to let your friends know you value reciprocity? I do not think so. Certainly, it is much more gracious to be open and share this value than it is to make excuses and stop seeing them altogether, especially when your ultimate goal is to stay in relationship.

Lavana, Valentyna, and I belong to a great group, The Three Angels. We delight in being present for each other, listening to worries, concerns, joys and successes. We also look for ways to give each other books, articles, and other items to soothe our souls. We really love being with each other and make a point of spending birthdays together in a relaxing location. Our trust for each other runs deep and the cornerstone of this trust is the reciprocity within the relationships.

Some people say "giving is receiving" and I can agree with this principle and still disagree with supporting one who only takes. In his book of daily meditations, the Dalai Lama states:

> If in a competitive society you are sincere and honest, in some circumstances people may take advantage of you. If you let someone do so, he or she will be engaging in an unsuitable action and accumulating bad Karma that will harm them in the future. Thus, it is permissible, with an altruistic motivation, to take counteraction in order to prevent the other person from having to undergo the effects of this wrong action. (Dalai Lama, *The Path to Tranquility-Daily Meditations,* New Delhi: Penguin Books, 1998. P.113.)

Clearly, when Bryan informed Steve that he was aware of his freeloading ways, he was preventing Steve from building up his bad Karma and saving him from an unhappy future. In addition, Bryan was saving himself from further bouts of resentment induced by taking more than his fair share of beer.

Chapter XVII

SELF DEVELOPMENT

*M*ANY PEOPLE ARE ON A QUEST TO FEEL
MORE SPIRITUALLY FULFILLED. WHEN WE
DEVELOP OUR CORE IDENTITY, WE DEVELOP
DEEP SPIRITUALITY.

Spirituality Is at the Centre of Being

True to the pattern throughout this book I have developed a prescription, a one-step formula, to fast-forward spiritual enlightenment. I first learned about this concept from George Addair at Omega Vector. He challenged me never to criticize anyone for breaking his or her word to me unless I was one hundred percent accountable for my word, to myself and to others.

How to Fast Forward Spiritual Development

When I hear someone state, "I am spiritual" I ask, "as compared to whom?" I believe that we are all spiritual in equal measure; that the addict living and mentally ill on the street are no less spiritual than any of us who meditate, do yoga, give back to the community, and live a religious life. It is just that some of us are more conscious and more in touch with our strengths. As I said before by quoting Ernest Hemmingway, "The world breaks all of us; some are stronger in the broken places." My personal belief is that everyone we meet carries has at least three problems weighing on his or her heart and shoulders at any one time. If I am tempted to compare myself to others, I remind myself of then and then I am more able to see the oneness between us rather than the separation.

Sign a Contract with Yourself

To lead a more spiritual life, with integrity to our true core, we must make a non-negotiable deal with ourselves. The wording of this contract should go something like this:

> *Whenever I give my word, or whenever I make a commitment, no matter how small or to whom, I will keep it one hundred percent. If something should come between my commitment and me, I will be one hundred percent accountable for breaking that commitment. I will take one hundred percent responsibility and re-negotiate. I know that if I am one hundred percent accountable and take one hundred percent responsibility for maintaining my commitments or renegotiating them, I will be one hundred percent trustworthy, and therefore well advanced in my spiritual life. From this moment on, this is my commitment to myself.*

Name: _____ Date: _____

In short, your agreement with yourself and the world is, "When I give my word I keep it. My word is my bond. If something comes between me and my word, I will advise the other and renegotiate a new outcome."

In maintaining this agreement you must become even more careful about your commitments because each commitment has to be either kept or renegotiated. Positive results will quickly appear when you do this.

The more I give my word, and keep it, the more trustworthy I become.

The respect and esteem with which others view you, and with which you view yourself, will increase dramatically. You will become a program of attraction. You will be able to tap into the good graces of others, achieving your goals and dreams with cleverness and effectiveness. You will appear to be lucky. All this, just by making that one change…these results, I promise to you.

Being Resilient

If you are resilient, you are one of the lucky ones who became strong at your broken places. As I typed the last sentence, I felt immense sadness was over my heart for those among us who just could not mend those hurts and injuries. The resilient ones are the lucky ones.

Life provides plenty of opportunities for us to do more and be more. We are meant to become mentally strong and emotionally resistant. It should take a hurricane, not a puff of wind, to blow us off course. When we show up big in our lives we must do so without blaming others, giving excuses or defending less than illustrious behavior. The result is that we become resilient people.

I like to think resilience is the capacity to take life on life's terms with an optimistic attitude, to adept in the face of adversity, to see more than one possible solution, and to develop social competence despite exposure to severe stress. Being resilient means moving away from victim mode to being *in agency* with your life where you stand in your own circle of power without the need or compulsion to wrestle power from others. When you have a forgiving heart, you will have a wealth of spiritual elegance and you will react to situations with equanimity and grace. When you slip and practice a maladaptive defense, as we all do from time to time, you will quickly take responsibility for your actions, make amends, and restore balance.

How resilient people demonstrate their resilience:

- They accept and appreciate people.
- They are dependable and do not shift the burden of blame or make someone else responsible for their peace of mind.
- They give more than they take.
- They detach from the drama of a problem and search to find the solution.
- They do not accept credit unless credit is due.
- They meet strangers easily.
- They ask questions and listen with interest.
- They can look at a situation from several points of view.
- They know their limitations and weaknesses and are not defined by them. They work to overcome both.
- They can manage emotions and feelings.
- They can work with others.
- They can establish and maintain personal boundaries.
- They face problems and issues squarely.
- They assume responsibility for their mistakes.
- They set goals and work toward them.
- They hold general feelings of goodwill toward others.

This is not to say resilient people are necessarily paragons of virtue. It is just that they are able to take life on life's terms without becoming co-opted by the vagrancies of life. Sometimes bad things happen to them but they do not become bitter or retaliatory. They maintain their equanimity and grace.

Personal Mastery

To be in agency for yourself is the key principle of personal mastery. Being in agency means: being able to detach in the moment, and to be an intelligent observer of oneself. Personal mastery allows you not to take the outbursts of others personally. It means developing the ability to investigate your own dramas with a real sense of ownership. The following ten steps will help you close the gap between what is happening now, and how you would like things to be:

Step #1: Practice Active Awareness

The practice of active awareness is fascinating. See yourself in your mind's eye observing a bothersome situation. Observe yourself feeling anger. See your fist clenching. See yourself as spiritually inelegant, getting your way by intimidation rather than by consensus. Observe how it feels to get your way by stealing power from another. Notice this feeling of power soon turns to powerlessness, and you are on the rampage again. Now imagine making a conscious choice to calm down, seeking to understand the other person's point of view. Consciously switch from an angry mode to your benevolent power and notice yourself telling the truth with grace and respect.

These good feelings remain evident long after the situation has been resolved. It is as if you mentally step back and think: *There I am in a situation and I see myself wanting to punch this person in the nose. No, I do not think I will do that. Instead, I will ask a question and possibly diffuse the moment.*

When you this on an ongoing basis, you will have a true sense of yourself. Your thinking, feeling and behavioral patterns will become clear. You will see just who you are under a variety of situations. This is a power-from-within process. Many martial arts practices end the class with a question asked by Sensei (leader), "Whom do we seek to overcome?" Of course, the answer is, "Myself!"

Observe yourself in various situations. If you are prone to be critical of others, have a conversation with yourself that goes something like this:

> *What I notice about me is that when I have more than two stresses in my life at one time, I become impatient and critical with others. It is as if I unknowingly take my stress and dump it onto them. They get my stress, and I get their peace of mind. Because this has become the normal transaction in our home, I cannot be much fun to be around. From now on, I must give myself time to be alone and to reflect on all the possible options before I react. So please, God (or your own version of a Higher Power), do not let me react now.*

The response we make to what we perceive to be true when we are in a victim state is less rational than the response we would make later. As the stresses build we can say to ourselves, "If I answer immediately I am likely to be critical, so I must ask for some time to think about this, and come back later with a well-thought out response and a variety of solutions."

Active awareness is a process that gives us the ability to observe ourselves at all times. We already know how to look outward at others and have discerning observations. Active awareness requires us to turn that process inside. Freud called this the "observant ego," meaning you can look at your thoughts, feelings, emotions, words, and behaviors and make choices to change them. Notice and observe your thoughts and feelings but do not judge them. Just notice them.

Over time, as you consistently, or even inconsistently, practice this process a pattern will emerge. You will know you, from the inside out. This sense of knowing enables you to see the values and behaviors you have that are unchanging, as if cast in stone. You also notice other things about you that vacillate and are malleable. This emerging sense of you is powerful. You might even think, *I am beginning to develop a feeling of resilience, assurance, and confidence. I know me! I have strengths and I have weaknesses. This gives me a sense of pride about my strengths, humility about my weaknesses, and pleasure about my brilliance. I am whole – a perfectly imperfect human being. On one hand I see my struggle with wanting to do the right thing, and on the other hand I sometimes see myself sometimes taking the easy way out and defaulting to old non-productive behaviors. However, more often than not, I see myself making the more productive (right) choice.*

This active self-awareness eventually builds a solid bridge of connection to who we actually are.

Step #2: Avoid Judgment and Practice Discernment

We've learned the difference between discernment and judgment. Judgment occurs when we create an opinion that has no room for flexibility and openness. We attach the morality of good or bad, rather than make an observation or statement of perception. An unchecked assumption is very close to a judgment. If I find myself judging, I quickly reverse the effects by saying, "Bless them; improve me!" This relieves me of the opportunity (as there always is in judging) to uphold a superior opinion of myself by putting someone else in an inferior spot, even for that one moment of comparison. It is impossible to notice a weakness in another without feeling superior. But to make myself feel important at the expense of someone else means that on some level I must be feeling inferior.

Discernment allows for the perceptions of others to flow and influence. A discerning comment might be, "I notice her behavior is often one way one day, and another way the next. I wonder what that means? I wonder what she is all about, and how does this affect me?" A judgmental comment might be, "She is erratic and undependable." This is certainly more closed than the first comment.

Step #3: Add Up the Cost of the Comfort Zone

Our victim selves are attached to the same old excuses and reasons we give ourselves for not moving out of the comfort zone (or perhaps our discomfort zone), because life is unpleasant when we do not have the power of choice over ourselves. When we need to do something good for ourselves but are afraid to, we absolutely believe some conjured-up, catastrophic outcome will occur. However, do not believe everything you think! Making resolutions and having great intentions but not following up on them destroys peace of mind.

It is better to do something imperfectly than not at all. This creates agency. Freedom comes with release from the fear, anxiety, and self-recrimination that accompanies avoidance.

Step #4: Monitor the Words You Say to Yourself

Supportive self-talk and the ability to remain gracious in a situation where you would normally fight, flee, freeze or comply, is an emotionally mature choice. For instance, if you are in the company of someone who is upset, you could say to yourself, "This is not about me," or "The poor soul is so upset over something that is fixable," or "I'm doing the best I can," or "My best will get better as a result of this experience."

Step #5: Eradicate Blaming

When you blame another person, you shift responsibility from you to the other person. That individual is now in charge of your outcomes. Blaming another person excuses you from taking responsibility. It is as if when we offer an excuse, we actually presume the other person will believe the excuse.

What if you enlist the help of a co-worker in good faith but this person lets you down? Their shortfall derails your project but all eyes are focused on you. Normally this situation would activate uncomfortable feelings. Instinct would have you releasing the uncomfortable feelings by blaming the co-worker who let you down. Why not do that? Because blaming, places you in the position of being victimized by your co-worker.

To maintain one hundred percent responsibility you might say to the project manager, "My portion of the project is due in one day and I need more time because circumstances that I did not foresee have developed."

Then go to work and fix as much as you can, as quickly as you can. To go on a witch-hunt would only delay the project putting you on the defensive and depleting your creative energy. Remember, you are the one who has the character trait of trusting the untrustworthy. Use this experience of being let down to develop your communication skills.

Step #6: Avoid Justifying and Defending Your Actions

Some people, when they are not busy blaming others, are justifying themselves. Have you ever used any of the following justifications?

- I didn't get to the reports because ...
- The department head would not help me repair the system, so I will not be able to complete the project on time.
- The estimator did not add travel time to the quote.
- The market is slow so business is slow.

We are arguing for our limitations when we justify our actions or attitudes. When confronted with information that hurts or angers, it is wise to objectively consider that feedback and ask, "Is there a grain of truth to what I am being told?"

Step #7: Avoid Defending Your Actions

Defending is defensive. People who defend themselves compare their behavior to that of others and can generally find reasons to be exactly where they are in life.

- I was fired because the boss is an idiot.
- Oh, yeah, you think I am bad. Well, you should hear yourself!
- I would not have done that if you had not made me so mad!

The two typical behavior patterns of not being accountable or responsible are blaming and shaming, and justifying and defending. Although exerting these defenses feels right in the moment, it can never lead to producing the long-term results you really want in your life. *When you defend a position you are actually arguing for a limitation!*

Step #8: Take Life on Life's Terms

When you practice behaviors that are congruent with agency, you will become resilient and in charge of your life, instead of becoming a victim. That is not to say there will not be difficult times. But if you take life on life's terms, you can use your energy more productively. The energy you would use to be frustrated and annoyed can instead be used to create a plan to get to a solution.

Step #9: Create a Work Plan

Have a mission and a vision, and measure every decision against it. If you do not have your own dream, someone else's dream will have to do. Have a plan and consistently work that plan. If you do not stand up for something of importance to you, there is a risk you will fall for everything.

Step #10: Develop the Qualities of Personal Mastery

It is vital that you set an action plan in place to develop the following traits. Although this is a partial list, it will get you started on the path to greater success.

Adaptable	Able to change easily to meet new circumstances.
Analytical	Able to determine the nature of a thing by separating it into its parts.
Articulate	Able to speak clearly and effectively in expressing thoughts and feelings.
Communicative	Able to connect with others by expressing and exchanging ideas effectively in speaking, writing, and listening.
Conceptual	Has the intellectual capacity to visualize an abstract idea.
Confident	Believes in one's abilities based on realistic self-assessment.
Cost Conscious	Constantly interested in increasing efficiency and economies of scale.
Decisive	Able to make decisions without procrastination based on assessing the best options in a situation. Willing to commit to a course of action based on carefully analyzed options communicating to all involved in the implementation.
Diplomatic	Able to reach a compromise or desired result through discussion, compromise, and consensus.
Discerning	Probing beneath the surface to get to the core of problems; testing findings in terms of data and facts; not accepting things at face value.

Detail Conscious	Exercises extreme care in the consideration or treatment of details.
Diligent	Applies steady, earnest effort to the performance of a task or objective.
Disciplined	Possesses the willpower to carry out tasks without procrastination.
Driven	Employs great energy and persistence in carrying an undertaking to completion.
Empathic	Possesses ability to place oneself in another's shoes.
Ethical	Acts with honesty and integrity, showing respect for the law, the rights of others, and the company's code of ethics.
Far-seeing	Possesses the ability to anticipate the future consequences of actions.
Flexible	Possesses the ability to adapt to a variety of situations, individuals, and groups; appreciates opposing perspectives of an issue; adapts to a dynamic business environment.
Hard-Working	Willing to stretch and work with extra effort to get the job done.
Impactful	Able to gain and hold the attention of others.
Innovative	Capable of introducing new ideas or methods to make changes that increase efficiency.
Intellectually Curious	Thirsty for knowledge; keenly interested in investigation and acquiring knowledge or information.
Motivated	Has the internal energy and drive to act to accomplish a goal.
Objective	Able to view facts with little or no distortion.
Open-Minded	Willing to consider new ideas or approaches.
Perceptive	Aware of the behavior of others that reveals their true feelings, attitudes, and intentions.

Personable	Possesses the combination of perceptivity, tact, empathy, and persuasiveness that enables one to get along well with and influence others.
Persuasive	Able to win others over to believing or doing something.
Productive	Able to accomplish a great deal of effective work.
Quality-Focused	Motivated to achieve superior results; interested in and appreciative of excellence.
Realistic	Capable of applying knowledge to some useful end. Thinks and acts objectively, and rejects what is impractical.
Reliable	Honors commitments.
Resourceful	Able to rise to the occasion by devising ways and means to solve a problem; able to improvise.
Responsible	Reliable and trustworthy; willing to be held accountable.
Responsive	Inclined to react promptly to suggestions and requests.
Results-Oriented	Has strong drive to accomplish a task or objective.
Risk-Taking	Willing to place oneself in circumstances of doubtful outcome and live with the consequences in pursuit of a valuable objective.
Safety-Conscious	Recognizes the criteria for a safe environment. Takes initiative to correct issues that expose self and others to unsafe practices.
Self-directed	Takes needed action before being asked or required, and does significantly more than is minimally required.
Tactful	Has a keen perception of what is fit; considerate in dealing with others to avoid offending.
Thorough	Carries to a conclusion any activity that has been planned and initiated.
Well-Timed	Perceives of the precise moment for doing something, or not doing something.

As you review this list, ask yourself an important question such as:

1. Where do I stand with each of these characteristics?
2. What do I need to do to improve on the traits that I want to have as part of my overall makeup?
3. Whose help do I need?

Remember, when we ask big questions we receive big answers, and we are never the same again.

Chapter XVIII

A COURTEOUS HEART

*I*t is vital to go through life with
a forgiving attitude. This applies to the
big things and the small.

Become Loving in the Present

Forgiving people and circumstances is the best technique for living in the moment and staying in the now. When you obsess about the past or worry about the future, you deplete your vital energy.

You develop a courteous heart when you go through life with a forgiving attitude. Because a courteous heart does not interfere with another's character, it may appear detached. This is not so. A courteous heart feels no need to criticize, regulate, or improve another person. It does not search for a reason to make others feel guilty. It does not say, "Why didn't you do that?" or, "You made me feel bad." A courteous heart simply looks at the other person or situation with discernment versus judgment.

A courteous heart knows that to judge is to limit its ability to learn. More than anything, it wants to be open to the experiences and gifts of others. A courteous heart knows that it cannot learn from someone it judges to be less than it is. A courteous heart knows recalling a hurtful event will instill fear and cause itself pain.

Having a courteous heart does not mean you will tolerate the intolerable, or accept the unacceptable. It means you will change what you can and let go of, or forgive the rest. If someone is in your face and you feel uncomfortable or want to retaliate, contain your emotions with the mantra, *God bless this person and improve me.* This releases the person to a power greater than you and frees you from the limiting emotion of judgment. It also causes you to admit to yourself that you, too, are imperfect, in need of help and blessings. Adopting a forgive and forget attitude frees you. It gives you more focus and energy to get off the other person's case, and to get on with your life. It frees the other person from being accountable to you.

Adopting a completely forgiving attitude does not mean you have no boundaries. Quite the reverse is true. However, when you do create a boundary it is elegant instead of defensive. The boundary you create is about the behavior, not about the person. When you attack a person, you lose your power.

If you do not let others know your boundaries, they may offend you by what they say or do. However, they are not responsible because you have not taken the time to identify your boundaries. If you have educated them, and they continue the offensive behavior, you will have to make a decision about whether to remain in contact.

Boundaries usually need to be emphasized and repeated a couple of times. If we have been in a relationship over an extended period without healthy boundaries, we essentially have taught our partner how to treat us. Our partner will not abandon this pattern without resistance! Your persistence in creating elegant boundaries will reduce this resistance to respecting your boundaries.

When you become angry while maintaining a boundary, you are effectively moving from a boundary to a defense. Typically, a defensive posture only stimulates more defenses – attack is met with attack; this is common. Notice how skilled our world powers are at attacking each other!

The gift you give yourself by going through life with a *forgive and forget attitude*, is that you develop a courteous heart, and you become spiritually elegant. One who is spiritually elegant does not feel snobbish or superior; is able to learn from everyone else. The divine spirit of the universe works through people, all kinds of people, from all kinds of lifestyles. A courteous heart embraces all and, therefore, experiences the divine in all, including the divine in ourselves. The positive results show.

A courteous heart allows you to stay more emotionally present by not holding onto the past with resentment and anger. Letting go of your fear places you in the current moment, not wishing for the future or looking to the past. Freeing up this energy creates an opportunity to live more fully in the now. This ability to remain exceptionally focused enables you to make decisions with greater clarity than ever before.

How often have you made choices based on your projection of the past onto the current situation? Why not live in the moment and choose according to what is actually going on right now? Just consider the lightness and joy created by being free of those old patterns of anger and resentment. When the forgiving, courteous heart has created an empty space where anger used to live, there will be room to fill that void with joy, laughter, and love. This is a conscious choice – to let go of something old, to clean out the garbage you were holding onto, to un-clutter your emotions and make room for new beginnings.

Something amazing happens when you truly forgive. There is an increase in our understanding of what it means to be human with all our frailty and all our strengths. When you can find it in your heart to accept and forgive others, you will discover that it becomes easier to forgive yourself for what you perceive are your own shortcomings. Many times, we are our own worst critic. Judgment of others and ourselves has succeeded in creating a world of limitations. Through forgiveness and letting go you will experience an increase in human compassion. This new love for all beings can open the door to a grand future filled with a level of peace and contentment that is unparalleled.

Looking back at your interactions with others you can be thankful for the wisdom and lessons a particular person or situation created so you could grow. When the cloud of anger has lifted simply acknowledge the benefit inherent in the experience and, where applicable, remember the love that originally attracted you to this person in the first place.

At this moment, you will be self-empowered. With this level of love and acceptance of your own self, you will not need to give your power to others to gain love or approval. Nor will you unnecessarily take the power from others to provide a sense of self that personal doubt had stolen from you. You will be totally secure within your own being and will not look to anyone else to create it for you. By opening our hearts, we receive the gift of inner peace and contentment. In my humble opinion, to live this way, with an open heart is as close as a human being can come to the state of divine spiritual love.

As you open your heart to practice forgiveness, you will experience the gift of inner peace.

There Is Nothing to Forgive

Forgiveness heals both the one who asked for and received forgiveness, and the one who forgave. As the saying goes, you have to give in order to get – or in this case, you have to for*give* in order to for*get*.

She said to him, "Forgive me for being who I am, and who I am not."

"Oh no," he replied. "It is I who needs forgiveness from you for being who I am, and who I am not."

It was then they experienced mutuality, and understood that with acceptance there is never anything to forgive.

CPSIA information can be obtained at www.ICGtesting.com
Printed in the USA
LVOW102040140413

328973LV00005B/17/P